Meet the Boxer

- The Boxer is classified by the American Kennel Club as a Working dog.

- Boxers descend from various larger breeds. The breed was developed in Germany using Bulldogs and some terriers.

- Boxers are said to have gotten their name from how they defended themselves. At the beginning of a fight with another dog, a Boxer would stand up on his hind legs and bat at his opponent, appearing to "box."

- Boxers particularly love children and are very protective of them.

- The Boxer is playful and patient and demanding of his owner's love and attention.

- The Boxer is capable of communicating his feelings with his face. His face wrinkles up into expressions of curiosity, excitement, happiness, surprise or sadness.

- The Boxer is well known for the coat colors fawn and brindle, both of which can be various shades.

- Boxers are naturally clean and frequently groom themselves in the same manner as cats.

- A quick weekly brushing takes care of the Boxer's grooming needs.

Consulting Editor
IAN DUNBAR PH.D., MRCVS

Featuring Photographs by
WINTER CHURCHILL
PHOTOGRAPHY

Howell Book House
An Imprint of Macmillan General Reference USA
A Pearson Education Macmillan Company
1633 Broadway
New York, NY 10019

Macmillan Publishing books may be purchased for
business or sales promotional use. For information
please write: Special Markets Department,
Macmillan Publishing USA, 1633 Broadway,
New York, NY 10019.

Library of Congress Cataloging-in-Publication
Data
            The essential boxer / consulting
editor, Ian Dunbar; featuring photographs by
Winter Churchill Photography.
            p.   cm.
    Includes bibliographical references and index.
    ISBN 1-58245-067-6
    1. Boxer (Dog breed).   I. Dunbar, Ian.
SF429.B75E77   1999   99-12403
636.73—dc21   CIP

Manufactured in the United States of America
10 9 8 7 6 5 4 3 2

Series Director: Michele Matrisciani
Production Team: David Faust, Clint Lahnen, Dennis
Sheehan, Terri Sheehan, Christina Van Camp
Book Design: Paul Costello

*Boxers featured in this book have been provided by:
Pam Rohr of Dreamweaver Boxers, Cheri Bush of
Synergy Boxers, and Texas Boxer Rescue.*

ARE YOU READY?!

☐ Have you prepared your home
and your family for your new
pet?

☐ Have you gotten the proper
supplies you'll need to care for
your dog?

☐ Have you found a veterinarian
that you (and your dog) are
comfortable with?

☐ Have you thought about how
you want your dog to behave?

☐ Have you arranged your schedule to accommodate your dog's
needs for exercise and attention?

*No matter what stage you're at with
your dog—still thinking about getting one, or he's already part of the
family—this Essential guide will
provide you with the practical information you need to understand and
care for your canine companion. Of
course you're ready—you have this
book!*

Boxer

The Boxer's Senses

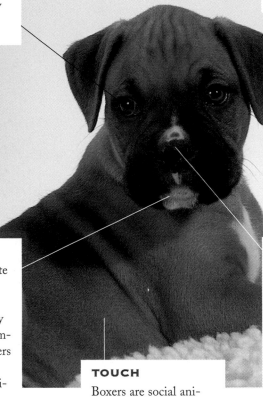

SIGHT

Boxers can detect movement at a greater distance than we can, while they can't see as well up close. They can also see better in less light, but can't distinguish many colors.

SOUND

Boxers, like all dogs, can hear about four times better than we can, and they can hear high-pitched sounds especially well.

TASTE

Boxers have fewer taste buds than we do, so they're likelier to try anything—and usually do, which is why it's important for their owners to monitor their food intake. Dogs are omnivorous, which means they eat meat as well as vegetables.

TOUCH

Boxers are social animals and love to be petted, groomed and played with.

SMELL

A Boxer's nose is his greatest sensory organ. A dog's sense of smell is so great, he can follow a trail that's weeks old, detect odors diluted to one-millionth the concentration we'd need to notice them and even sniff out a person underwater!

CHAPTER ONE

Getting to Know Your Boxer

A Boxer is a complicated animal. More than any other dog, his moods mirror those of his master. His sensitivity is astonishing. While he is a great clown, always ready to run and play, he can display great courage and even aggression when needed. His eyes are almost human in their expression, and in them you can clearly read his state of mind.

The Boxer is often the very definition of "independence." While he may mellow with advanced age, a Boxer is a physically active dog. He loves to roughhouse—he will fetch an object and cheerfully dare his owner to take it back. He will refuse to move over if you attempt to push him aside. He has a tendency to jump up, and there is considerable

muscular force behind these loving greetings.

BOXERS PLAY HARD

This agile leaping is no doubt a part of his genetic heritage: His name itself evolves from the German "Boxen," or "Boxer." Though it cannot be definitely proven, the name probably derives from the Boxer's habit of playing with his front paws. He uses these paws almost like hands: to poke and punch. Females, after giving birth, use their front paws to cradle their young.

One cannot underestimate a Boxer's strength. He is quite capable of knocking an adult man to his knees. It is therefore imperative to train a Boxer to curb his natural

It is thought that Boxers got their name because they use their paws like hands.

tendencies to leap and make body contact. Remember—he was bred to overpower large animals, so these instincts come quite naturally to your Boxer.

Until he is trained, your Boxer will also have an instinctive desire to pull on his leash; he could easily drag you down the street. It is obvious that he must be firmly instructed in "civilized" behavior. He is not a dog for the proverbial "little old lady"—until he knows his manners.

BOXERS GET BORED

Training your Boxer can be a challenge. You will find that he is of superior canine intelligence. This intellect, combined with his independence, demands a strong trainer, one wise in the ways of such dogs. First, we must remember that a Boxer gets bored very easily. While he can be quickly taught everything from polite behavior to parlor tricks, he will not perform reliably if he sees no point to the exercise.

Boredom may be mistaken for stubbornness by the unwary trainer. Therefore, instructing a Boxer must be made "fun" for the dog; he must

2

look forward to these sessions, not dread them. Most (not all) trainers employ edible treats and much praise to enhance these exercises. Gradually, as the dog consistently obeys, praise replaces the goodies. And in time, certain learned behaviors, such as walking in a responsive fashion on a lead, become simple second nature to the dog.

While I have called your attention to the Boxer's physical strength, it must be said that all his clownish and rough-and-tumble ways are usually tempered with good judgment. While he may gallop right at you, as if to mow you down, he will turn aside at the last delicious moment.

BOXERS LOVE KIDS

He is apt to be gentler and less bold with women than with men, and when a Boxer meets children, magic happens. Boxers adore children. If you walk a Boxer down a crowded street, you will invariably find that his attention is engaged by kids of all shapes and sizes. He finds them fascinating creatures, and in your household he will almost always be found at the side of the littlest

3

Boxers are very protective of children.

people around. Your Boxer will take any amount of abuse from a child without a thought of retaliation. Indeed, he will seem to thrive on the sometimes careless games that a child may invent for his dog—the 2-year-old's "Let's pour sand in his ear" or "Let's pull his tail" game, or the 7-year-old's "Let's dress Rover up in mom's clothes" antics.

Boxers seem to understand instinctively the physical limitations of kids—from tiny tots to teens. Babies are regarded with the utmost respect,

Boxers are intelligent, clean, fun and extremely loving. What more could you want in a pet?

and you may often find your Boxer parked soulfully next to a crib, gently contemplating the infant therein.

Boxers are very protective of children, and many a mother has left her toddler briefly in a Boxer's care while her back was turned, secure in the knowledge that no harm would come to the baby if the dog was nearby. Indeed, your Boxer will have a special regard for all humans he understands to be helpless or handicapped—not only kids, but also the sick and infirm.

BOXER BEHAVIOR

A boxer has a great sense of humor. His antics around the house are a constant source of amusement to his human guardians. A Boxer is one of the few dogs who enjoys playing all by himself. If no human is available, he may pick up a toy or a tissue from the wastebasket (beware—wastebaskets are regarded as a Boxer's private "stash!") and parade around the house, tossing his prize not-so-delicately in the air and rolling over on it on the rug. You may return from an afternoon's shopping and find said rug swept to one side on the floor, and a Boxer greeting you with an impish glint in his eyes. Or, as in the case of a friend of ours, you may find your shoes tossed down the stairwell, a gesture clearly designed to tell you you've been absent too long!

A Boxer has an instinctive desire to be clean. He will groom himself constantly in a catlike fashion, licking off offending dirt, and using his paws to wipe his face. This natural tendency is easily channeled into quick and easy housebreaking for the young puppy. Contrary to popular myth, a Boxer does not drool any more than most dogs. In fact, the

only time he will do so is if he is constantly rewarded by begging food at the table. A Boxer does, however, accumulate water in his flews when drinking, and if he happens to shake his head soon after, onlookers beware!

A Boxer is a jealous dog. He is insistent and demanding of your affection, and thus, he is jealous of every living creature who could come between him and his family members. If one Boxer tries to curl up on your lap (an interesting feat!), you will

Boxers are demanding of their families' affection.

Boxers get along with other pets, although they prefer the company of their owners.

have two Boxers vying for the same space; if the family cat gets a pat on the head, the Boxer will insist on his due. He is also jealous and possessive about objects such as toys and food dishes. If a dozen rubber "squeakies" are scattered about the rug, you can count on two Boxers coveting the same latex mouse. Likewise, food dishes are zealously guarded.

CHARACTERISTICS OF THE BOXER

Sensitive

Courageous

Athletic

Easily bored

Loves children

Playful

Clean

BOXERS ARE NOT NOISY

One of the Boxer's great virtues is his relative silence. If you attend a Boxer national specialty (a dog show of just Boxers), you will be struck by the lack of canine noise you hear. That is not to say that your Boxer has no voice. Rather, he has a loud, booming, almost roaring bark when he feels the need to warn. He simply uses his vocal capabilities sparingly and only after thinking the situation over. Known as a "hearing guard dog," he will generally bark when a stranger enters his yard or another dog dares to cross his boundary line. Thus, he is a very effective watchdog. If the stranger is invited in, he will most likely become your Boxer's best friend, but we try not to publicize that fact in "Burglar World!"

Boxers are revered for their excellent watchdog abilities.

THE BOXER IN A NUTSHELL

Boxers are at once fun, frustrating, lovable, obstinate, uncannily bright and great clowns. They will make your home a happier place. When we lose them, as we inevitably must, we shall remember the morning they stole a pound of butter from the kitchen; we shall remember the tails that wagged with delight every time they saw us; we shall remember their sweetly quizzical expressions, and their unquestioning love.

No Boxer owner will ever attempt to equate "obedience" with "intelligence." A Boxer basically does what he does when he feels like doing it—but he learns like lightning. A Boxer needs to know why he should do something, why he should interrupt his leisure to pursue some silly human desire. If you give him reason enough, the Boxer just may perform for you—and do it in style. But a Boxer without a reason is a Boxer immovable.

7

CHAPTER TWO

Homecoming

A Boxer puppy will bring you untold joy—and she will try your patience. She will interrupt your sleep and wreak havoc with your daily routine. She will walk through her water and sit up on the rug. But she will also snuggle up beside you, lick your face and tell you in all her extensive Boxer vocabulary that you are the greatest human on earth. She will help make life worth living.

Choosing a puppy is usually a happy expedition to a breeder's home or kennel. Do not be put off if your puppy's owner puts you through the "third degree," asking questions like, "Where will the puppy sleep? Where will the puppy stay while you're at work? Do you have a fenced-in yard? If you owned a dog before, what happened to her?" All of these questions are designed to determine whether yours is a suitable home for the sweet puppy.

PICKING YOUR PUPPY

We shall assume you pass the "test" easily. Now, which puppy in the litter will be yours? The breeder may offer you a choice of only one or two. That's perfectly all right. There are very likely to be "reservations" for one or more of the babies—people who left deposits even before birth. Excellent breeders are sometimes booked well in advance of whelping.

If you do have a choice, be sure to pick a lively, alert animal, one who bounces up to greet you and wants to interact with the family. Do not be taken by the shy, shivering pup in the corner, no matter how "sorry" you may feel for her. Remember—she was raised under the same conditions as her littermates, and for reasons unknown to you, has not developed into a happy, well-adjusted animal. This could be temporary, due to a curable illness, or it could

This adorable Boxer waits patiently to be adopted from her rescue foster home.

be genetic, meaning that she may grow to be an unhappy adult.

Before bringing home your new family member, do a little planning to help make the transition easier. The first decision to make is where the puppy will live. Will she have access to the entire house or be limited to certain rooms? A similar consideration applies to the yard. It is simpler to control a puppy's activities and to housetrain the puppy if she is confined to definite areas. If doors do not exist where needed, baby gates make satisfactory temporary barriers.

A dog crate is an excellent investment and is an invaluable aid in raising a puppy. It provides a safe, quiet place where a dog can sleep. If it's used properly, a crate helps with housetraining. However, long periods of uninterrupted stays are not recommended—especially for young puppies. Unless you have someone at home or can have some-

Chew toys are an excellent diversion for a teething puppy.

one come in a few times a day to let her out to relieve herself and socialize with her for a while, a *small* crate is not advisable. Never lock a young puppy in a small crate for an entire day!

Make sure your Boxer will have company and companionship during the day. If the members of your family are not at home during the day, try to come home at lunchtime, let your puppy out and spend some time with her. If this isn't possible, try to get a neighbor or friend who lives close by to come spend time with the puppy. Your Boxer thrives on human attention and guidance, and a puppy left alone most of the day will find ways to get your attention, most of them

not so cute and many downright destructive.

ACCESSORIES

The breeder should tell you what your puppy has been eating. Buy some of this food and have it on hand when your puppy arrives. Keep the puppy on the food and feeding schedule of the breeder, especially for the first few days.

Your puppy will need a close-fitting nylon or cotton-webbed collar. This collar should be adjustable so that it can be used for the first couple of months. A properly fit collar is tight enough that it will not slip over the head, yet an adult finger fits easily under it. A puppy should never wear a choke chain or any other adult training collar.

In addition to a collar, you'll need a 4-to-6-foot-long leash. One made of nylon or cotton-webbed material is a fine and inexpensive first leash. It does not need to be more than a $^1/_2$ inch in width. It is important to make sure that the clip is of excellent quality and cannot become unclasped on its own. You will need one or two leads for walking the dog, as well as a collar or harness. If you live in a cold climate, a sweater or jacket for

PUPPY ESSENTIALS

To prepare yourself and your family for your puppy's homecoming, and to be sure your pup has what she needs, you should obtain the following:

Food and Water Bowls: One for each. We recommend stainless steel or heavy crockery—something solid but easy to clean.

Bed and/or Crate Pad: Something soft, washable and big enough for your soon-to-be-adult dog.

Crate: Make housetraining easier and provide a safe, secure den for your dog with a crate—it only looks like a cage to you!

Toys: As much fun to buy as they are for your pup to play with. Don't overwhelm your puppy with too many toys, though, especially the first few days she's home. And be sure to include something hollow you can stuff with goodies, like a Kong.

I.D. Tag: Inscribed with your name and phone number.

Collar: An adjustable buckle collar is best. Remember, your pup's going to grow fast!

Leash: Style is nice, but durability and your comfort while holding it count, too. You can't go wrong with leather for most dogs.

Grooming Supplies: The proper brushes, special shampoo, toenail clippers, a toothbrush and doggy toothpaste.

Do not buy chew toys composed of compressed particles, as these particles disintegrate when chewed and can get stuck in the puppy's throat. Hard rubber or plastic toys are also good for chewing, as are large rawhide bones. Avoid the smaller chew sticks, as they can splinter and choke the puppy. Anything given to a dog must be large enough that it cannot be swallowed.

The final starter items a puppy will need are a water bowl and food dish. You can select a smaller food dish for your puppy and then get a bigger one when your dog matures. Bowls are available in plastic, stainless steel and even ceramic. Stainless steel is probably the best choice, as it is practically indestructible. Nonspill dishes are available for the dog that likes to play in her water.

PUPPY-PROOFING

Outside

If you do not have a fenced yard, it would be useful to provide at least an outside kennel area where the puppy could safely relieve herself. Failing that, the youngster should be walked outdoors on a lead several

Boxer puppies need human companionship and shouldn't be left alone for long periods of time.

excursions with your Boxer would be appropriate. Get a somewhat larger size than you immediately need to allow for growth.

Excessive chewing can be partially resolved by providing a puppy with her own chew toys. Small-size dog biscuits are good for the teeth and also act as an amusing toy.

A dog crate will provide your Boxer with a safe place to rest or play.

times a day, taking care at first that the lead is sufficiently tight around her neck so that she cannot slip out of it.

Inside

You will also need to puppy-proof your home. Curious puppies will get into everything everywhere. Even if you generally keep your Boxer close to you or in her indoor or outdoor enclosure, there will be times when she wants to explore and you cannot watch her. Make sure your home has been puppy-proofed so you can be reasonably confident she won't do serious damage to herself or your home.

Securely stow away all household cleaners and other poisonous products, such as antifreeze, which,

IDENTIFY YOUR DOG

It is a terrible thing to think about, but your dog could somehow, someday, get lost or stolen. For safety's sake, every dog should wear a buckle collar with an identification tag. A tag is the first thing a stranger will look for on a lost dog. Inscribe the tag with your dog's name and your name and phone number.

There are two ways to permanently identify your dog. The first is a tattoo, placed on the inside of your dog's thigh. The tattoo should be your Social Security number or your dog's AKC registration number. The second is a microchip, a rice-sized pellet that is inserted under the dog's skin at the base of the neck, between the shoulder blades. When a scanner is passed over the dog, it will beep, notifying the person that the dog has a chip. The scanner will then show a code, identifying the dog.

It is important to provide your pet with an adjustable collar and an identification tag.

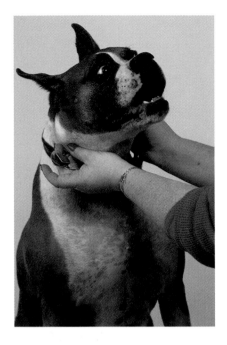

unfortunately, has a taste dogs seem to love. Keep all electrical cords out of reach, and secure electrical outlets.

Make sure you have removed poisonous plants from your house and garden. Puppies put everything into their mouths, and you need to make sure there's nothing dangerous they can get into. Inside, dangerous plants include poinsettia, ivy and philodendron. Outside, holly, hydrangea and azalea are among the plants of which your puppy should steer clear. The bulbs and root systems of daffodils, tulips and others are also poisonous.

Boxers need scheduled time for playing, exercising, eating and sleeping.

THE ALL-IMPORTANT ROUTINE

Most puppies do best if their lives follow a schedule. They need definite and regular periods of time for playing, eating and sleeping. Puppies like to start their day early. This is a good time to take a walk or play some games of fetch. After breakfast, most are ready for a nap. How often this pattern is repeated will depend on one's daily routine. Sometimes it is easier for a working person to stick with a regular schedule than it is for someone who is home all of the time.

Most dogs reach their peaks of activity and need the least amount of rest from 6 months to 3 years of age. As they mature, they spend increasingly longer periods of time sleeping. It is important to make an effort to ensure that a Boxer receives sufficient exercise each day to keep her in proper weight and fitness throughout her life. Puppies need short periods of exercise, but, because their bodies are developing, they should never be exercised to excess.

HOUSEHOLD DANGERS

Curious puppies and inquisitive dogs get into trouble not because they are bad, but simply because they want to investigate the world around them. It's our job to protect our dogs from harmful substances, like the following:

In the Garage

antifreeze

garden supplies, like snail and slug bait, pesticides, fertilizers, mouse and rat poisons

In the House

cleaners, especially pine oil

perfumes, colognes, aftershaves

medications, vitamins

office and craft supplies

electric cords

chicken or turkey bones

chocolate, onions

some house and garden plants, like ivy, oleander and poinsettia

15

CHAPTER THREE

To Good Health

Boxers, with good care, commonly live ten to twelve or more years. When health problems do arise, your dog's best line of defense is *you*— the loving, alert owner who will see to it that proper medical treatment is rendered early and effectively.

CHOOSING A VETERINARIAN

You will find that your choice of veterinarian is critical to your dog's good care. This practitioner must not only be skilled as a diagnostician and a surgeon, but must also be a good listener—to you, as you know your dog best. Beware the vet who never has time to talk to you, or doesn't care what you have to say. Beware the vet who constantly belittles your medical expertise. The best medical professionals will be acutely interested in your observations and your insights. Seek recommendations from experienced breeders in your area; they will offer very definite opinions on who you should trust to do the right thing in a time of crisis. They may know that a particular vet has a particular knowledge of or love for the Boxer breed. All this advice is helpful, but the final choice is yours. Be sure you have confidence in your vet, that he or she is medically skilled and is someone to whom you can relate.

THE IMPORTANCE OF PREVENTIVE CARE

You can help your dog maintain good health by practicing the art of preventive care. Take good care of your Boxer today and he will be healthy tomorrow.

There are many aspects of preventive care with which Boxer owners should be familiar: vaccinations, regular vet visits and tooth care are just some.

The earlier that illness is detected in the Boxer, the easier it is for the veterinarian to treat the problem. Owners can help ensure their dogs' health by being on the lookout for

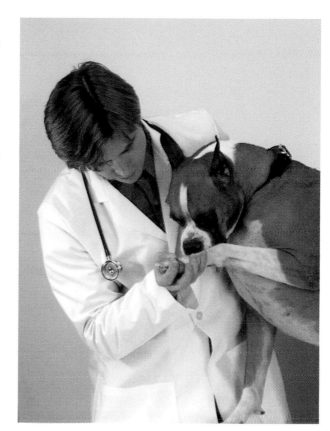

17

medical problems. All this requires is an eye for detail and a willingness to observe. Pay close attention to your Boxer, how he looks, how he acts. What is normal behavior? How does his coat usually look? What are his eating and sleeping patterns? Subtle changes can indicate a problem. Keep close tabs on what is normal for your Boxer, and if anything

Your Boxer should feel comfortable with his veterinarian.

out of the ordinary develops, call the veterinarian.

Vaccinations

A priority on a Boxer owner's list of preventive care is vaccinations. Vaccinations protect the dog against a host of infectious diseases, preventing an illness itself and the misery that accompanies it.

Vaccines should be a part of every young puppy's health care, since youngsters are so susceptible to

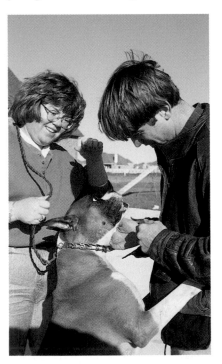

Boxers are affectionate and enjoy making new friends.

disease. To remain effective, vaccinations must be kept current.

Good Nutrition

Dogs that receive the appropriate nutrients daily will be healthier and stronger than those that do not. The proper balance of proteins, fats, carbohydrates, vitamins, minerals and sufficient water enables the dog to remain healthy by fighting off illness.

Routine Checkups

Regular visits to the veterinary clinic should begin when your Boxer is a young pup and continue throughout his life. Make this a habit and it will certainly contribute to your Boxer's good health. Even if your Boxer seems perfectly healthy, a checkup once or twice a year is in order.

Well-Being

Aside from the dog's physical needs—a proper and safe shelter, nutritious diet, health care and regular exercise—the Boxer needs plenty of plain, old-fashioned love. The dog is happiest when he is part of a family, enjoying the social interactions, nurturing and play. Bringing the Boxer into the family provides the dog with a sense of security.

The Boxer needs mental stimulation as well, especially because the breed is so intelligent. Obedience training is an excellent way to encourage your dog to use his mind. Remember, Boxers will use their brilliant minds in some manner, so it is best to direct them in a positive way.

COMMON DISEASES

Unfortunately, even with the best preventive care, the Boxer can fall

YOUR PUPPY'S VACCINES

Vaccines are given to prevent your dog from getting infectious diseases like canine distemper or rabies. Vaccines are the ultimate preventive medicine: They're given before your dog ever gets the disease so as to protect him from the disease. That's why it is necessary for your dog to be vaccinated routinely. Puppy vaccines start at 8 weeks of age for the five-in-one DHLPP vaccine and are given every three to four weeks until the puppy is 16 months old. Your veterinarian will put your puppy on a proper schedule and will remind you when to bring in your dog for shots.

19

Maintaining your Boxer's health means keeping vaccinations current.

ill. Infectious diseases, which are commonly spread from dog to dog via infected urine, feces or other body secretions can wreak havoc. Following are a few of the diseases that can affect your Boxer.

Rabies

Since rabid animals may have a tendency to be aggressive and bite, animals suspected of having rabies should only be handled by animal control handlers or veterinarians.

Rabies is preventable with routine vaccines, and such vaccinations are *required by law* for domestic animals in all states in the U.S.

One of the most well-known diseases that can affect dogs, rabies can strike any warm-blooded animal (including humans)—and is fatal. The rabies virus, which is present in an affected animal's saliva, is usually spread through a bite or open wound. The signs can be subtle at first. Normally friendly pets can become irritable and withdrawn. Shy pets may become overly friendly. Eventually, the dog becomes withdrawn and avoids light, which hurts the eyes of a rabid dog. Fever, vomiting and diarrhea are common.

Once these symptoms develop, the animal will die; there is no treatment or cure.

Parvovirus

Canine parvovirus is a highly contagious and devastating illness. The hardy virus is usually transmitted through contaminated feces, but it can be carried on an infected dog's feet or skin. It strikes dogs of all ages and is most serious in young puppies.

There are two main types of parvovirus. The first signs of the diarrhea-syndrome type are usually depression and lack of appetite, followed by vomiting and the characteristic bloody diarrhea. The dog appears to be in great pain, and he usually has a high fever.

The cardiac-syndrome type affects the heart muscle and is most common in young puppies. Puppies with this condition will stop nursing, whine and gasp for air. Death may occur suddenly or in a few days. Youngsters that recover can have lingering heart failure that eventually takes their life.

Veterinarians can treat dogs with parvovirus, but the outcome varies.

It depends on the age of the animal and severity of the disease. Treatment may include fluid therapy, medication to stop the severe diarrhea and antibiotics to prevent or stop secondary infection.

Young puppies receive some antibody protection against the disease from their mother, but they lose it quickly and must be vaccinated to prevent the disease. In most cases, vaccinated puppies are protected against the disease.

Coronavirus

Canine coronavirus is especially devastating to young puppies, causing depression, lack of appetite, vomiting that may contain blood and characteristically yellow-orange diarrhea. The virus is transmitted through feces, urine and saliva, and the onset of symptoms is usually rapid.

Dogs suffering from coronavirus are treated similarly to those suffering from parvovirus: fluid therapy, medication to stop diarrhea and vomiting and antibiotics if necessary.

Vaccinations are available to protect puppies and dogs against the virus and are recommended especially for those dogs in frequent contact with other dogs.

Hepatitis

Infectious canine hepatitis can affect dogs of every age, but it is most severe in puppies. It primarily affects the dog's liver, kidneys and lining of

ADVANTAGES OF SPAYING/NEUTERING

The greatest advantage of spaying (for females) or neutering (for males) your dog is that you are guaranteed your dog will not produce puppies. There are too many puppies already available for too few homes. There are other advantages as well.

Advantages of Spaying

No messy heats.

No "suitors" howling at your windows or waiting in your yard.

No risk of pyometra (disease of the uterus) and decreased incidences of mammary cancer.

Advantages of Neutering

Decreased incidences of fighting, but does not affect the dog's personality.

Decreased roaming in search of bitches in season.

Decreased incidences of many urogenital diseases.

PREVENTIVE CARE PAYS

Using common sense, paying attention to your dog and working with your veterinarian, you can minimize health risks and problems. Use vet-recommended flea, tick and heartworm preventive medications; feed a nutritious diet appropriate for your dog's size, age and activity level; give your dog sufficient exercise and regular grooming; train and socialize your dog; keep current on your dog's shots; and enjoy all the years you have with your friend.

the blood vessels. Highly contagious, it is transmitted through urine, feces and saliva.

Infectious canine hepatitis must be diagnosed and confirmed with a blood test. Ill dogs require hospitalization. Hepatitis is preventable in dogs by keeping vaccinations current.

Lyme Disease

Lyme disease has received a lot of press recently, with its increased incidence throughout the United States. The illness, caused by the bacteria *Borrelia burgdorferi,* is carried by ticks. It is passed along when the tick bites a victim, canine or human. (The dog cannot pass the disease to people, though. It is only transmitted via the tick.)

In dogs, the disease manifests itself in sudden lameness, caused by swollen joints, similar to arthritis. The dog is weak and may run a fever. The lameness can last a few days or several months, and some dogs have recurring difficulties.

Antibiotics are very effective in treating Lyme disease, and the sooner it is diagnosed and treated, the better. A vaccine is available; ask your veterinarian if your dog would benefit from it.

Kennel Cough

"Kennel cough" or "canine cough," is a contagious disease that shows itself as a harsh, dry cough. It has been termed "kennel cough" because of its often rapid spread through kennels. The cough may persist for weeks and is often followed by a bout of chronic bronchitis.

Three types of ticks (l–r): the wood tick, brown dog tick and deer tick.

Many kennels require proof of bordatella vaccination before boarding. If your dog is in and out of kennels frequently, vaccination certainly is not a bad idea.

MEDICAL CONDITIONS SPECIFIC TO BOXERS

Despite all our care and attention, our Boxers do occasionally suffer from conditions to which the breed seems to be predisposed. Whether these illnesses are genetic in origin or occasioned by environmental factors, they nonetheless need to be addressed.

Cancer

Boxers have been found to be at high risk for a large variety of tumors. These include both benign skin tumors as well as cancers affecting the brain, skin, thyroid, mammary glands and testes and internal organs, such as the spleen and pancreas. Benign skin tumors usually need either no treatment or simple surgical removal under local anesthesia. Malignancies require treatment specific to

WHEN TO CALL THE VETERINARIAN

In any emergency situation, you should call your veterinarian immediately. Try to stay calm when you call, and give the vet or the assistant as much information as possible before you leave for the clinic. That way, the staff will be able to take immediate, specific action when you arrive. Emergencies include:

- Bleeding or deep wounds
- Hyperthermia (overheating)
- Shock
- Dehydration
- Abdominal pain
- Burns
- Fits
- Unconsciousness
- Broken bones
- Paralysis

Call your veterinarian if you suspect any health troubles.

the cancer itself and vary widely. As in human cancers, dogs are treated with surgery, chemotherapy and sometimes radiation.

Gingival Hyperplasia

These are benign tumors of the mouth, mainly an overgrowth of gum tissue, commonly seen in middle-aged and older Boxers. These tumors may be numerous; however, they usually cause no significant harm. Occasionally, they distort the placement of the lips and are cosmetically unattractive. Since they may catch and hold food particles, the owner must pay attention to oral hygiene. Always consult your veterinarian to rule out any potential malignancy.

Paying attention to your Boxer's oral hygiene will help you monitor his gums for signs of gingival hyperplasia.

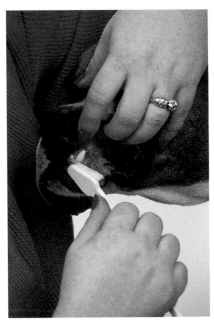

Heart Disease

Like most breeds of dogs, Boxers are subject to heart ailments. These include congenital anomalies as well as acquired disease later in life. Boxer heart disease usually falls into two categories: aortic stenosis and cardiomyopathy.

Hip Dysplasia

This is a developmental disease of the hip joint affecting many breeds of dogs, including Boxers. The head of the femur (thigh bone) and the acetabulum (hip socket) become incompatible; the joint weakens and loses proper function. Reluctance to engage in strenuous physical activity, lameness and pain are all possible signs of hip dysplasia, usually manifested between the ages of 4 months to 1 year. Stair climbing or rising from a sitting or lying position may be difficult, and the dog may cry out if the hip joint is manipulated. Radiographs are definitively diagnostic and will show evidence of abnormal joint laxity. Treatment is aimed at relieving symptoms of pain and includes drug therapy and surgery. Hip dysplasia is believed to be hereditary, but other factors such as diet and conditioning cannot be ruled out. Dogs older than 24 months can be evaluated by and registered with the Orthopedic Foundation for Animals (OFA) in Columbia, Missouri (see chapter 9 for the address).

Hypothyroidism (Thyroid Deficiency)

The onset of hypothyroidism in the adult Boxer is becoming more commonly diagnosed. Hypothyroidism may be caused by thyroid tumors or a primary malfunction of the gland. Symptoms may include excessive hair thinning and loss, obesity, anemia, reproductive failures and infertility and lethargy. Diagnosis is confirmed by testing the blood and confirming inadequate levels of circulating thyroid hormones. The administration of carefully determined doses of replacement hormone will alleviate most symptoms and will probably need to be given for the balance of the dog's life.

FIRST AID

First aid is not a substitute for professional care, though it can help save a dog's life.

To Stop Bleeding

Bleeding from a severe cut or wound must be stopped right away. There are two basic techniques—direct pressure and the tourniquet.

Try to control bleeding first by using direct pressure. Ask an assistant to hold the injured Boxer and place several pads of sterile gauze over the wound. Press. Do not wipe the wound or apply any cleansers or ointments. Apply firm, even pressure. If blood soaks through the pad, do not remove it as this could disrupt clotting. Simply place another pad on top and continue to apply pressure.

If bleeding on a leg or the tail does not stop by applying pressure, try using a tourniquet. Use this only as a last resort. A tourniquet that is left on too long can result in limb loss.

A dog's curiosity will often lead him to eat or lick things he shouldn't.

Regular veterinary checkups, daily exercise, balanced nutrition and a lot of old-fashioned TLC will help keep your Boxer happy and healthy.

26

If the dog is bleeding from his mouth or anus, or vomits or defecates blood, he may be suffering from internal injuries. Do not attempt to stop bleeding. Call the veterinarian right away for emergency treatment.

POISON ALERT

If your dog has ingested a potentially poisonous substance, waste no time. Call the National Animal Poison Control Center hot line:

(800) 548-2423 ($30 per case) or

(900) 680-0000 ($20 first five minutes; $2.95 each additional minute)

Shock

Whenever a dog is injured or is seriously ill, the odds are good that he will go into shock. A decreased supply of oxygen to the tissues usually results in unconsciousness; pale gums; weak, rapid pulse; and labored, rapid breathing. If not treated, a dog will die from shock. The conditions of the dog should continue to be treated, but the dog should be as comfortable as possible. A dog in shock needs immediate veterinary care.

Poisoning

Unfortunately, many substances are poisonous to dogs, including household products, plants or chemicals. Owners must learn to act quickly if poisoning is suspected because the results can be deadly.

If your dog appears to be poisoned:

- Call your veterinarian and follow his or her directions.

- Try to identify the poison source—this is really important. Take the container or plant to the clinic.

- Induce vomiting if you are sure the dog has ingested a poisonous substance, and if you are sure the substance is not kerosene, turpentine, drain cleaner, tranquilizers or sharp objects, or that more than two hours has passed since the poison was swallowed.

- Do not try to induce vomiting in a semi- or unconscious animal.

- Transport the dog to the clinic as directed by the vet. Bring with you the telephone number for the National Animal Poison Control Center (see sidebar in this chapter for more information).

Heatstroke

Heatstroke can be deadly and must be treated immediately to save the dog. Signs include rapid panting, darker-than-usual gums and tongue, salivating, exhaustion or vomiting. The dog's body temperature is elevated, sometimes as high as 106°F. If the dog is not treated, coma and death can follow.

If heatstroke is suspected, cool down your overheated dog as quickly as possible. Mildly affected dogs can be moved to a cooler environment, into an air-conditioned home, for example, or wrapped in moistened

towels. Call your veterinarian immediately.

Insect Bites/Stings

Just like people, dogs can suffer bee stings and insect bites. Bees, wasps and yellow jackets leave a nasty, painful sting, and if your dog is stung repeatedly, shock can occur.

If an insect bite is suspected, try to identify the culprit. Remove the stinger if it is a bee sting, and apply a mixture of baking soda and water to the sting. It is also a good idea to apply ice packs to reduce inflammation and ease pain. Call your veterinarian, especially if your dog seems ill or goes into shock.

27

You take on a lot of responsibility when deciding to own a Boxer puppy—but it is well worth it.

WHAT'S WRONG WITH MY DOG?

We've listed some common symptoms of health problems and their possible causes. If any of the following symptoms appear serious or persist for more than 24 hours, make an appointment to see your veterinarian immediately.

CONDITIONS	POSSIBLE CAUSES
DIARRHEA	Intestinal upset, typically caused by eating something bad or over-eating. Can also be a viral infection, a bad case of nerves or anxiety or a parasite infection. If you see blood in the feces, get to the vet right away.
VOMITING/RETCHING	Dogs regurgitate fairly regularly (bitches for their young), whenever something upsets their stomachs, or even out of excitement or anxiety. Often dogs eat grass, which, because it's indigestible in its pure form, irritates their stomachs and causes them to vomit. Getting a good look at *what* your dog vomited can better indicate what's causing it.
COUGHING	Obstruction in the throat; virus (kennel cough); roundworm infestation; congestive heart failure.
RUNNY NOSE	Because dogs don't catch colds like people, a runny nose is a sign of congestion or irritation.
LOSS OF APPETITE	Because most dogs are hearty and regular eaters, a loss of appetite can be your first and most accurate sign of a serious problem.
LOSS OF ENERGY (LETHARGY)	Any number of things could be slowing down your dog, from an infection to internal tumors to overexercise—even overeating.

28

INTERNAL PARASITES

Dogs are susceptible to several internal parasites. Keeping your Boxer free of internal parasites is another important aspect of health care.

Watch for general signs of poor condition: a dull haircoat, weight loss, lethargy, coughing, weakness and diarrhea.

For proper diagnosis and treatment of internal parasites, consult a veterinarian.

CONDITIONS	POSSIBLE CAUSES
STINKY BREATH	Imagine if you never brushed your teeth! Foul-smelling breath indicates plaque and tartar buildup that could possibly have caused infection. Start brushing your dog's teeth.
LIMPING	This could be caused by something as simple as a hurt or bruised pad, to something as complicated as hip dysplasia, torn ligaments or broken bones.
CONSTANT ITCHING	Probably due to fleas, mites or an allergic reaction to food or environment (your vet will need to help you determine what your dog's allergic to).
RED, INFLAMED, ITCHY SPOTS	Often referred to as "hot spots," these are particularly common on coated breeds. They're caused by a bacterial infection that gets aggravated as the dog licks and bites at the spot.
BALD SPOTS	These are the result of excessive itching or biting at the skin so that the hair follicles are damaged; excessively dry skin; mange; calluses; and even infections. You need to determine what the underlying cause is.
STINKY EARS/HEAD SHAKING	Take a look under your dog's ear flap. Do you see brown, waxy build-up? Clean the ears with something soft and a special cleaner, and don't use cotton swabs or go too deep into the ear canal.
UNUSUAL LUMPS	Could be fatty tissue, could be something serious (infection, trauma, tumor). Don't wait to find out.

29

Roundworms

Roundworms, or ascarids, are probably the most common worms that affect dogs. Most puppies are born with these organisms in their intestines, which is why youngsters are treated for these parasites as soon as it is safe to do so.

Animals contract roundworms by ingesting soil and feces, or by ingesting chicken, rodent or other animal tissues that are contaminated with roundworm eggs. A roundworm infestation can rob vital nutrients from young puppies and cause diarrhea, vomiting and digestive upset. Roundworms can also harm a young animal's liver and lungs, so treatment is imperative.

Tapeworms

Tapeworms are commonly transmitted by fleas to dogs. Tapeworm eggs enter the body of a canine host when the animal accidentally ingests a carrier flea. The parasite settles in the intestines, where it sinks its head into the intestinal wall and feeds off material the host is digesting. The worm grows a body of egg packets, which break off periodically and are expelled from the body in the feces. Fleas then ingest the eggs from the feces and the parasite's life cycle begins all over again.

Hookworms

Hookworms are so named because they hook onto an animal's small intestine and suck the host's blood. Like roundworms, hookworms are contracted when a dog ingests contaminated soil or feces.

Hookworms can be especially devastating to dogs. They will become thin and sick; puppies can die. An affected dog will suffer from bloody diarrhea and, if the parasites migrate to the lungs, the dog may contract bronchitis or pneumonia.

Hookworms commonly strike puppies 2 to 8 weeks of age and are less common in adult dogs.

Whipworms

Known for their thread-like appearance, whipworms attach into the wall of the large intestine to feed. Thick-shelled eggs are passed in the feces and in about two to four weeks are mature and able to reinfect a host that ingests the eggs.

Mild whipworm infestation is often without signs, but as the worms grow, weight loss, bloody diarrhea and anemia follow. In areas where the soil is heavily contaminated, frequent checks are advised to prevent severe infestation.

Heartworms

Heartworms are transmitted by the ordinary mosquito, but the effects are far from ordinary. Infection begins when the larvae from an infected mosquito are laid on the dog's skin. They burrow into the skin, or are ingested when the dog licks. In three to four months, the larvae (microfilaria) become small worms and make their way to a vein, where they are transported to the heart. The worms burrow into the heart, grow and reproduce.

At first, a dog with heartworms is free of symptoms. The signs vary, but the most common is a deep cough and shortness of breath. The dog tires easily, is weak and loses weight. Eventually, the dog may suffer from congestive heart failure.

EXTERNAL PARASITES

FLEAS—Besides carrying tapeworm larvae, fleas bite and suck the host's blood. Their bites itch and are extremely annoying to dogs, especially if the dog is hypersensitive to the bite. Fleas must be eliminated on the dog with special shampoos and dips. Fleas also infest the dog's bedding and the owner's home and yard.

TICKS—Several varieties of ticks attach themselves to dogs, where they burrow into the skin and

FLEAS AND TICKS

There are so many safe, effective products available now to combat fleas and ticks that—thankfully—they are less of a problem. Prevention is key, however. Ask your veterinarian about starting your puppy on a flea/tick repellent right away. With this, regular grooming and environmental controls, your dog and your home should stay pest-free. Without this attention, you risk infesting your dog and your home, and you're in for an ugly and costly battle to clear up the problem.

31

suck blood. Ticks can be carriers of several diseases, including Lyme disease and Rocky Mountain Spotted Fever.

LICE—Lice are not common in dogs, but when they are present they cause intense irritation and itching. There are two types: biting and sucking. Biting lice feed on skin scales, and sucking lice feed on blood.

MITES—There are several types of mites that cause several kinds of mange, including sarcoptic, demodectic and cheyletiella. These microscopic mites cause intense itching and misery to the dog.

THE AGING BOXER

Geriatric Boxers require the same amount of attention and care as younger dogs.

Canine geriatric medicine has made great advances over the years. Full and happy lives can often be prolonged by appropriate medical treatments designed to rejuvenate and relieve the stress from failing organ systems.

Symptoms of Aging

While most Boxers tend to act youthful all their lives, your elder statesman may decline to run and play as he once did. He may develop arthritis; if he suffered any skeletal or joint injuries in his life, they may begin to cause him discomfort. He may have difficulty rising or exhibit intermittent lameness. There are excellent pain remedies for these problems that can be prescribed by your veterinarian.

Your own responsibilities to the geriatric dog are mostly a matter of good common sense. He should not be allowed to become obese. If your Boxer seems inclined to tear around as if he were a puppy, but you know that he has a fragile knee joint or spinal arthritis or a bad heart, limit his exercise within sensible parameters. Give him a nice soft bed to lie on. And above all, keep up his grooming, keep his toenails trimmed and make him feel that he is still a valued member of the household.

CHAPTER FOUR

Positively Nutritious

The importance of good feeding is obvious, but the rules for maintaining a dog on good food and a sensible feeding regimen are wonderfully simple. It is when dog owners start making up their own rules about feeding that good husbandry can become derailed.

Dog owners take their pets to the veterinarian when they become ill, to the groomer for a special occasion or to a training session when the spirit moves them. However, they feed their pets every single day. What they are fed, when they are fed and how they are fed are of great importance.

Over the course of a dog's life, her nutritional requirements will change just as ours do, and it is

Your Boxer's nutritional needs should be first on your priority list.

important to be aware of those needs ahead of time. If you approach the entire matter of feeding from a commonsense point of view and arm yourself with good information, you can expect that your dog will be properly fed for her entire life.

FEEDING YOUR BOXER PUPPY

If you are about to get your first Boxer, you will surely want to know just what to do to make sure you feed her properly. Before you bring her home, ask what she is being fed and when, and stick to the same food and routine after you get her home. Do this for at least the first week or so.

In most cases, the puppy you get will be on three meals a day. Stick to this number of feedings as much as possible. A Boxer puppy will continue to grow until she is about 9 months old, and it is important to feed with this fact in mind. You may need to change feeding times to accommodate your own lifestyle. No problem. Just make sure that you ease the puppy into your requirements. Making abrupt changes can be stressful and physically upsetting for the puppy.

The three-meals-a-day routine should be followed until the puppy reaches about 6 months of age. At this point, put her on a morning and an evening meal until she reaches her first birthday. At a year of age, she will do well on one meal a day, with biscuits in the morning and at bedtime. However, if you prefer to keep your Boxer on two meals a day, there is no reason not to.

WHAT TO FEED YOUR BOXER

Today, we and our dogs benefit from extensive research that has been conducted to find the best foods available for routine, day-to-day feeding, as well as foods for growing puppies, geriatrics, dogs with specific health needs and dogs with high levels of activity. The various dog food companies have gone to considerable expense to develop nutritionally complete, correctly balanced diets for all dogs. Feeding the right amount of a high-quality food should suffice. That may, however, be easier said than done, as owners often have an emotional tendency to enhance their pets' food, often to the detriment of the dog (more on this subject later in the chapter).

Dry Food (Kibble)

The basis of your dog's diet should be dry kibble. A high-quality, well-balanced kibble is nutritionally complete and will be relished by your dog under all normal conditions. Most major dog food companies manufacture a special formulation to meet the explosive growth of young puppies. These are highly recommended for daily feeding up to your Boxer's first birthday. Use the puppy foods. They work! For a mature dog, choose a kibble with a minimum of 20 percent protein. This and other important nutritional information will be on the label.

GROWTH STAGE FOODS

Once upon a time, there was puppy food and there was adult dog food. Now there are foods for puppies, young adults/active dogs, less active dogs and senior citizens. What's the difference between these foods? They vary by the amounts of nutrients they provide for the dog's growth stage/activity level.

Less active dogs don't need as much protein or fat as growing, active dogs; senior dogs don't need some of the nutrients vital to puppies. By feeding a high-quality food that's appropriate for your dog's age and activity level, you're benefiting your dog and yourself. Feed too much protein to a couch potato and she'll have energy to spare, which means a few more trips around the block will be needed to burn it off. Feed an adult diet to a puppy, and risk growth and development abnormalities that could affect her for a lifetime.

FOOD ALLERGIES

If your puppy or dog seems to itch all the time for no apparent reason, she could be allergic to one or more ingredients in her food. This is not uncommon, and it's why many foods contain lamb and rice instead of beef, wheat or soy. Have your dog tested by your veterinarian, and be patient while you strive to identify and eliminate the allergens from your dog's food (or environment).

Puppies and adolescent dogs require a higher intake of protein, calories and nutrients than adult dogs.

Many experienced dog keepers are firm believers in feeding dry kibble, or just flavoring it slightly with broth or canned meat to heighten palatability. Others, just as adamantly, insist that the dog is a natural meat eater and her diet should contain significant amounts of fresh or canned meat. Actually, a diet that mixes both meat and kibble is likely to provide your dog with the best features of both foods. If one had to come down on the side of one food or the other, the winner would have to be an all-kibble diet. Studies have shown that dogs raised on all-meat diets often suffer from malnutrition and serious deficiencies, which may cause extreme physically debilitating problems.

Adding Canned Food or Meat

If you decide to add meat to the food, the best choice is beef. It may be freshly cooked, if you like, or canned. There are some very fine canned meats available, and it is a good idea for you to check the label, looking for about 10 percent protein. Chicken is also a good food source and is available in canned form. If you cook any poultry for your Boxer, bone it carefully. The same is true for fish, which most dogs relish. Cottage cheese is another good protein source, especially for puppies or dogs convalescing from illness.

Water

Besides feeding a high-quality food, you must keep ample clean, fresh water available for your dog at all times. It is vital to do so.

ESTABLISHING A FEEDING SCHEDULE

Establishing a feeding schedule depends on the demands of your own daily routine. Whatever time you decide, feed at the same time every day. Dogs are creatures of habit and are happiest when maintained on a specific schedule. Of course, there will be days when you can't be there to feed your pet at her regular dinner hour. It's okay. An occasional break in the routine is not a disaster, as long as your dog knows that most of the time she will be fed at a set time.

HOW MUCH TO FEED YOUR BOXER

The amount of food you feed your Boxer depends on the individual dog: her age, health, stage of life and activity level.

If your Boxer is very active, she will burn more calories and need more food than a house pet who doesn't get extraordinary amounts of exercise. There will be a difference in the eating patterns of a growing puppy and an elderly animal. If your dog is ill or convalescing, her food needs will also differ from the requirements of a healthy animal. Use your own educated judgment.

If a healthy dog cleans her bowl but still appears hungry, she might

TO SUPPLEMENT OR NOT TO SUPPLEMENT?

If you're feeding your dog a diet that's correct for her developmental stage and she's alert, healthy looking and neither over- nor underweight, you don't need to add supplements. These include table scraps as well as vitamins and minerals. In fact, unless you are a nutrition expert, using food supplements can actually hurt a growing puppy. For example, mixing too much calcium into your dog's food can lead to musculoskeletal disorders. Educating yourself about the quantity of vitamins and minerals your dog needs to be healthy will help you determine what needs to be supplemented. If you have any concerns about the nutritional quality of the food you're feeding, discuss them with your veterinarian.

With a tummy full of puppy food, this Boxer pre- pares for a mid- afternoon nap.

need a little more to reach the right amount of daily ration. Adjust accordingly.

Another way to determine whether you are feeding the right amount of food is to let the dog's condition tell you. If your dog is healthy but appears thin, you may want to feed a bit more. If the dog looks to be on the plump side, a more restricted diet is in order. If you can't feel your dog's ribs beneath her fur, she's overweight. Weigh your dog, get your vet's advice and start her on a diet right away.

HOW MANY MEALS A DAY?

Individual dogs vary in how much they should eat to maintain a desired body weight—not too fat, but not too thin. Puppies need several meals a day, while older dogs may need only one. Determine how much food keeps your adult dog looking and feeling her best. Then decide how many meals you want to feed with that amount. Like us, most dogs love to eat, and offering two meals a day is more enjoyable for them. If you're worried about overfeeding, make sure you mea- sure correctly.

Whether you feed one or two meals, only leave your dog's food out for the amount of time it takes her to eat it—ten minutes, for example.

THE PICKY EATER

A healthy dog will eat food when it's offered and most of the time will clean the dish. If you know your Boxer is healthy, but she consistently refuses to eat the good food you put in front of her, don't get into the habit of pampering her by offering alternative foods. This will only stif- fen her resolve. Feed her at the same time and in the same quiet place every day. Leave the food down for five minutes and then remove it en- tirely, whether she has eaten or not. Don't worry, a healthy dog will eat before she starves.

FEEDING TWO OR MORE DOGS

If you have to feed two or more dogs, crates can be useful. In multiple-dog households, each dog should eat in her own crate—with the door locked. In this way, each dog will eat in comfort, without being threatened by another dog in the household. This also helps you monitor how much each dog eats daily. In the absence of separate crates, dogs should be fed where others in the home cannot get at their food.

Although enhancing your Boxer's diet by adding people food is perfectly acceptable, make sure to insist on impeccable table manners.

39

PEOPLE FOOD

It can be okay to offer human food at times and to add table scraps occasionally to your dog's food, but do it wisely and in moderation. Dogs like carrots, broccoli and other fresh vegetables; some even like fruits.

These are okay, as are bits of cooked meat (no bones). And remember all those balanced rations mentioned earlier in this chapter: Quality food made specifically for dog feeding will do a better job of nourishing your pet than treats you may feel good about offering.

CHAPTER FIVE

Putting on the Dog

Grooming your Boxer, as you might imagine, is not a complicated effort. Affectionately known as "wash and wear" dogs, they require no involved grooming procedures. The requirements for keeping your Boxer clean and happy are simple.

You will find it helpful to train your Boxer from puppyhood to stand quietly while you are performing simple grooming tasks. If you are able to work in one particular area, your Boxer will quickly become accustomed to his routine. While it is not necessary, the purchase of a grooming table—a sturdy, nonskid surface on strong metal legs—will be easiest on your own back and eyes, and will tell your Boxer wherever you go that it is time for his regular grooming sessions. These tables fold up and can be easily packed in the car when you are traveling with your dog.

BRUSHING AND BATHING

A Boxer's coat is short and sleek. It is the very devil to remove from clothing and upholstered surfaces, as the little hairs seem to have a willful desire to stick to the most unwelcome places. Your Boxer will shed these hairs with regularity, and if you live in a cold weather area, he will shed almost his entire coat in what will appear like a spring moult! Therefore, a curry comb made of firm rubber, applied in a circular motion, will help you to remove the dead hair coat before it ends up all over you and the upholstery. Be sure that the curry comb is not too hard and that you apply it gently so as not to irritate his sensitive skin.

Your Boxer will need very few baths in his lifetime. He is a naturally clean animal, licking himself in catlike fashion to keep himself tidy and polished. Frequent bathing will remove essential oils from your dog's coat and can result in irritation. Any minor surface dirt can be easily whisked away with the use of a soft

41

The "wash and wear" Boxer is an easy dog to keep clean.

This woman is using a hound glove to remove loose hairs from her Boxer's coat.

glove or washcloth. If circumstances demand a bath (for example, your Boxer encountered a fully functioning skunk or decided to roll in cowpies!), you will want to make sure above all that your dog stays warm throughout the process and does not become chilled. Choose a hot summer day outdoors or a heated bathroom for the procedure. Be sure to dry your dog thoroughly with clean toweling.

When bathing your Boxer, select a mild dog shampoo. If you are bathing to kill fleas, be sure that your veterinarian approves the insecticidal soap you use; some medicated shampoos are toxic not only to the fleas but

Boxers don't take naturally to water—good thing they don't need baths too often!

After working the shampoo into a lather, be sure to thoroughly rinse all traces of soap from your Boxer's coat.

to the dog as well! First, wet your dog thoroughly with warm water; do not shock him with water either too cold or too hot. Apply your chosen soap conservatively, rub it gently into a lather and rinse thoroughly. If un-rinsed soap dries on your dog's coat, it will look like dandruff and will certainly defeat the purpose for which the Boxer was bathed in the first place!

Always be careful to avoid getting soap in your dog's eyes. Even if it is not painful to them, it is certainly an irritant. Likewise, try to keep water out of your Boxer's ears—remember, he has no convenient ear "flap" to shed water. If you wish, you can gently swab the inside of the ears with cotton balls dampened with warm water or specially formulated ear cleaner. Do *not* go deep into the ear, as serious damage could be done to the delicate mechanism within.

TRIMMING TOENAILS

Regular trimming of your dog's toe-nails is essential. Untrimmed nails lead to splayed feet and will cause

This owner carefully clips her Boxer's toenails, avoiding the quick.

QUICK AND PAINLESS NAIL CLIPPING

This is possible if you make a habit out of handling your dog's feet and giving your dog treats when you do. When it's time to clip nails, go through the same routine, but take your clippers and snip off just the ends of the nail—clip too far down and you'll cut into the "quick," the nerve center, hurting your dog and causing the nail to bleed. Clip two nails a session while you're getting your dog used to the procedure, and you'll soon be doing all four feet quickly and easily.

Chewing on hard treats is a fun and simple way for your Boxer to keep his teeth and gums healthy.

your dog to slip on smooth surfaces. They also look terrible! If you begin gentle trimming on the young puppy, you should have no trouble continuing to trim all through your Boxer's adult life. Your puppy's breeder undoubtedly trimmed nails from the very earliest weeks in the whelping box, so your Boxer may already know the routine.

CHECKING TEETH AND GUMS

You can gently brush your Boxer's teeth with a soft human toothbrush, or a canine brush available at pet supply stores. You can use baking soda and water or one of the commercially available canine toothpastes. Do not be alarmed if you see an overgrowth of gum tissue in the older Boxer; this is most probably a benign condition rather common to the breed (see "Gingival Hyperplasia" in chapter 3).

If your Boxer has regular access to rubber, nylon or rope chew toys, and if he gets occasional hard-baked food treats (biscuits), you will usually find that the simple stimulus of chewing will keep his mouth and teeth healthy, and that tartar deposits remain at a minimum.

CHAPTER SIX

Measuring Up

Y ou have decided to share your life with a Boxer, one of the most engaging breeds in dogdom. She will return all the love and affection you give—and then some. She will protect you; she will make you laugh on the darkest days; and she will outwit you when she feels the need. Her loyalty will astonish you; her energy will exhaust you; and always her devotion will be constant.

THE STANDARD FOR THE BOXER

All purebred dogs are bred to a particular "standard," a type of blueprint of the breed (for more, see the "What Is a Breed Standard?" box). The most recent revision of the Official Breed Standard of the Boxer was adopted by the American Kennel Club on May 1, 1989.

WHAT IS A BREED STANDARD?

A breed standard—a detailed description of an individual breed—is meant to portray the ideal specimen of that breed. This includes ideal structure, temperament, gait, type—all aspects of the dog. Because the standard describes an ideal specimen, it isn't based on any particular dog. It is a concept against which judges compare actual dogs and breeders strive to produce dogs. At a dog show, the dog that wins is the one that comes closest, in the judge's opinion, to the standard for its breed. Breed standards are written by the breed parent clubs, the national organizations formed to oversee the well-being of the breed. They are voted on and approved by the members of the parent clubs.

Several parts of the written standard warrant some detailed discussion and explanation. Descriptions in quotation marks are from the official standard.

Despite a current fashion to breed taller Boxers, the standard tells us that the Boxer "is a medium-sized, square built dog," and further defines "medium-sized" as: "Adult males— 22 to 25 inches; females—21 to 23 inches at the withers. Preferably, males should not be under the minimum nor females over the maximum."

Boxers are not disqualified or even penalized for slight deviations from these ideals, but major departures are undesirable.

The Boxer's head is a distinctive feature of the breed.

Head

The standard says, "The chiseled head imparts to the Boxer a unique individual stamp." The essence of breed type in the Boxer is embodied in her head—from the bone structure to the mood-mirroring quality of her eye expression to the formation of her lips and chin. The head is what sets her apart from other breeds and is what those who know her think of as beautiful. To the uninitiated, the Boxer head may appear bizarre, but it was

46

developed to allow her to do the job that man required of her historically. She had to be able to catch and hold game until her master caught up to her. While her jaws, by necessity, had to have great strength, she also had to be able to breathe with her mouth embedded in thick folds of hide and fur. These requirements were satisfied by her head's unique structure.

Muzzle

"The beauty of the head depends on the harmonious proportion of muzzle to skull." The muzzle should be two-thirds the width of the skull and one-third the length of the head from the occiput to the tip of the nose. The occiput is the slightly rounded bony protuberance between the ears. Skin wrinkles appear on the forehead and contribute to the Boxer's unique, slightly quizzical expression. They are desirable but should not be excessive (referred to as "wet").

Eyes

The Boxer's eyes are a dark brown color—the deeper shades preferred. They must not be yellowish ("bird of prey" eyes). Neither should they be too round or owlish, nor too small. They reflect the dog's moods to an extraordinary degree, which the new owner will soon learn to his or her advantage.

Ears

Adding to the characteristic appearance of the breed in the U.S. are the Boxer's ears, which are usually "cropped"—surgically trimmed and shaped to stand upright. If you don't

In combination, the Boxer's eyes and wrinkles create an expression—a "look"— that is uniquely the breed's.

This gal sports natural or "uncropped" ears.

crop, somewhat tapering and long, enhances the expression.

Skull

The Boxer's skull is slightly arched on top, not too flat nor rounded. "The forehead shows a slight indentation between the eyes and forms a distinct stop with the topline of the muzzle." One of the most important features of the Boxer's head is that the "tip of the nose should lie slightly higher than the root of the muzzle." In other words, the nose should tip up slightly. Historically, it is essential in a correct head so that the dog may breathe while holding her prey. Note that the "tip-up" is very visible in profile. Note also that the muzzle protrudes slightly in front of the nose, further ensuring the ability to breathe. The shape of the muzzle is influenced by the "formation of both jawbones . . . through the placement of the teeth . . . and . . . through the texture of the lips."

Jaws

The Boxer is undershot; that is, the lower jaw protrudes beyond the

plan to show your Boxer, ear cropping is optional, and is in fact prohibited in the U.K. and discouraged in other parts of Europe. Ears are cropped most commonly when the puppy is between 6 and 12 weeks old. As the Boxer was originally bred to catch and hold game—sometimes wild boar and other sizable prey—it was desirable that she not have long, flapping, easily wounded ears. What began as a purely utilitarian practice ultimately became the fashion. As the AKC standard says, the ears are "set at the highest points of the sides of the skull." An attractive upper jaw "and curves slightly upward," ideally with "the corner upper incisors fitting snugly back of the lower canine teeth," giving the Boxer an almost unshakable grip. "The front surface of the muzzle is broad and squarish." The canine teeth beneath the full lips contribute greatly to this look. They should be wide apart in both upper and lower jaws. The row of lower incisors should be straight, while the upper incisors should be slightly convex. The distance between upper and lower jaws should be definitive but not so pronounced as to ever show teeth or tongue when the mouth is closed. A wry mouth—where upper and lower jaws are slightly askew and out of line with each other—is a very serious fault. The lips meet evenly in front. They are padded and thick, and the upper lip is supported by the canines of the lower jaw beneath. The Boxer's chin must be prominent and visible both from the front and in profile.

Body

A natural athlete, the Boxer is designed for speed and endurance when required, reflecting her origins as a

The Boxer's jaws were designed to give her "an almost unshakable grip."

hunter, as well as her modern roles of guard and companion dog. While an "elegant" appearance, especially in the show ring, is attractive and often desirable, she must never be "weedy." Never must there be anything less than an impression of real "substance"—the natural consequence of strong bone and superbly conditioned muscle.

When we say that the Boxer is a "square" dog, we mean the following: A vertical line drawn from the highest point of the withers to the ground should equal a horizontal line drawn

THE AMERICAN KENNEL CLUB

Familiarly referred to as "the AKC," the American Kennel Club is a nonprofit organization devoted to the advancement of purebred dogs. The AKC maintains a registry of recognized breeds and adopts and enforces rules for dog events including shows, obedience trials, field trials, hunting tests, lure coursing, herding, earth-dog trials, agility and the Canine Good Citizen program. It is a club of clubs, established in 1884 and composed, today, of over 500 autonomous dog clubs throughout the United States. Each club is represented by a delegate; the delegates make up the legislative body of the AKC, voting on rules and electing directors. The American Kennel Club maintains the Stud Book, the record of every dog ever registered with the AKC, and publishes a variety of materials on purebred dogs, including a monthly magazine, books and numerous educational pamphlets. For more information, contact the AKC at the address listed in Chapter 9, "Resources."

from the foremost projection of the chest (sternum) to the rear projection of the upper thigh. To achieve squareness, the Boxer cannot be long through the loin or the back. If she does exhibit these faults, she will inevitably look "long," and the square, balanced appearance that is an essential feature of the breed will be lost.

Neck

That balance is further characterized by the neck being of adequate length and exhibiting an elegant arch as it blends smoothly into the withers (the highest point of the shoulders).

Topline

The Boxer's topline—the back—is firm and straight, and slopes slightly to the croup.

Tail

The tail is set on high, "carried upward." Customarily it is docked, and anyone who has witnessed the furiously wagging tail of a happy Boxer will see the wisdom of docking. Not only would the long tail be a menace to furniture and toddlers, it would also be subject to injury and trauma. Docking is carried out when puppies are only a few days old. At the same time, front dewclaws (vestigial claws a few inches above the paw) are removed to prevent their snagging and tearing later in life.

Chest and Forechest

The chest and forechest are "well defined." The brisket must reach to the elbows. "The depth of the body at the lowest point of the brisket equals half the height of the dog at the withers." If this depth is not achieved, the Boxer will look slimmer and less substantial than she should. The deep chest allows ample room for heart and lungs and contributes to endurance during strenuous physical activity. The ribs are well-defined but not shaped like a barrel so as to give a rotund appearance. The lower line of the stomach is noticeably arched in "a graceful curve to the rear." This is simply referred to as "tuck up."

The Boxer is always alert to strange noises or occurrences.

51

Hindquarters

The angulation of the bones of the hindquarters must be in balance with the angulation of the shoulder assembly. "The upper arm is long, approaching a right angle to the shoulder blade." The rear quarters are well-angulated at the stifle (the "knee").

Gait

The balance of front and rear angulation of the bones allows the Boxer to cover ground in a smooth, effortless stride, with her back level and "adequate reach to prevent interference" of the front legs with the driving rear. This essential structure of front and rear is designed to give the Boxer maximum power to chase and maneuver. A stilted, inefficient gait results when inadequate angulation of the front and rear quarters prevents the Boxer's ideal, ground-covering reach and drive.

Colors

The Boxer's acceptable colors are fawn (shades of tan) and brindle ("clearly defined black stripes on a fawn background"). Brindling may be sparse, with only a few stripes, to exceedingly heavy, where the fawn background barely shows at all. This is known as "reverse" brindling. Both colors are equally acceptable. They are enhanced by attractive white markings, which "must not exceed one-third of the entire coat." In other words, if you could imagine the dog laid out like a bearskin rug, the white markings, including those on the stomach, must not exceed one-third of the body area.

This fawn Boxer gives a hug to her owner.

Typically, white markings occur on the face in the form of a blaze and/or a portion of white on the muzzle. If the dog has white markings on the face, they will "replace a part of the otherwise essential black mask." The dog may also have varying amounts of white on her front and rear legs, and a white chest and throat. White should not occur on the stifle or on the back of the torso proper, nor should it be so excessive on the face as to detract from "true Boxer expression." Totally white or almost totally white Boxers are not uncommon in a litter of puppies. Members of the American Boxer Club are pledged not to register or sell these puppies. Nor should they ever be bred, as to do so will alter the essential color patterns in the breed. While they are ineligible to compete in the show ring, they can be exhibited in obedience trials.

Character

The character and temperament of the Boxer make her unique among dogs. She is "instinctively a hearing guard dog." This means that she is always alert to strange noises or unusual occurrences that she might perceive as a threat to either herself or her family. A Boxer should be fearless, ready to defend and protect. Above all, however, a Boxer loves people—especially children. She is a boisterous, happy dog, always ready for a game or a romp in the woods. She responds with delight to "friendly overtures honestly rendered." No longer a hunter of boar or bear, she is happiest with the family that she will love beyond measure.

The Boxer is playful and loving with her family and friends.

53

CHAPTER SEVEN

A Matter of Fact

T he Boxer's origins are ancient. His ancestors can be traced back to the Assyrians (2300–600 B.C.), who used war dogs with "heavy heads, wide short muzzles, powerful build, and great courage" (*The Boxer*, by John P. Wagner, New York: Orange Judd Publishing Co., 1953). These animals were used by hunters to run down and hold game—bear, boar and bison.

In Germany, these heavy "Bullenbeissers" (bull biters) were held in great esteem, and "throughout the Middle Ages the Bullenbeisser was Germany's only hunting hound" *(ibid.)*. With the advent of the Napoleonic wars, the old ducal estates disbanded, boar and bear hunting almost ceased and a preference for a less ponderous Bullenbeisser ensued. This fashion also satisfied a growing demand for agile fighting dogs, popular in England and the Continent.

ESTABLISHING THE BOXER

By selecting for type and function, breeders developed a smaller and lighter dog from the purest old Bullenbeisser bloodlines. The modern Boxer and English Bulldog are a result of this process.

In the 1830s, the English exported to Germany a particular dog they called at the time a Bulldog but who was an animal rather resembling a small Mastiff. This dog appears twice in the pedigrees of early German Boxers, and with his genes came the white color and markings that had

hitherto been unknown in the Bullenbeisser. He may also have been useful in fixing head type in the Boxer.

In 1896, the first Boxer club, called the Deutscher Boxer Club, was formed in Munich. Other German Boxer clubs followed. The first German breed standard was written and adopted in 1902. In 1905, all the German clubs combined and approved the Munich Standard and Stud Book.

Though the Boxer's use as a fearless hunter gradually declined, he was valued in the nineteenth century as a participant in the cruel sport of bullbaiting. Many a spectator lost and won large sums betting on the

It's hard to believe that the ancestors of the devoted and loving Boxer were once used as fearless hunters and fighting dogs.

outcome of such contests. The Boxer would hold on to the bull's nose with fierce intent, and the bull would attempt to dislodge the dog by any means possible. Terrible injuries to both dog and bull resulted, and the "sport" was eventually banned.

The development and refinement of the breed—until the 1940s, when the U.S. became involved in

The beautiful Boxer is also a regal protector.

a meaningful way—must be credited to the Germans. The early German breeders exhibited their dogs in shows after the formation of their Boxer clubs, and a detailed record of their pedigrees exists so that we can see the clear ancestry of the modern Boxer from about 1890. In Germany many breeders contributed to the breed in those early days of record-keeping, but in America no one has had so great an influence as the famous von Dom kennels of Philip and Friederun Stockmann.

THE VON DOM BOXERS

The first von Dom Boxer was registered in Germany in 1911. From modest beginnings, and with considerable travail, Frau Stockmann bred some of the finest Boxers the world had yet seen. Her devotion to her dogs was legendary, and she worked tirelessly to keep them fed and warm in an increasingly politically unstable Germany.

Both Philip Stockmann and several of the von Dom standards were sent to the front lines when World War I broke out. The Munich Boxer Club initially sent sixty Boxers to the war effort. These dogs were used both to guard prisoners and as sentries. In addition, they would sometimes be sent out to catch and bring down an enemy soldier—actions harking back to their earlier hunting exploits in the forest.

The first von Dom connection to the U.S. was made in 1914 when Philip Stockmann returned from a show in Hamburg and announced to his wife that he had sold his dog Dampf von Dom after he had been awarded the "Sieger" (championship) title. At only 18 months of age, Dampf was imported to America, to the then-governor of New York, Herbert H. Lehman.

Unfortunately, because so few Boxer bitches existed in this country at the time, Dampf was not often used as a stud dog. He was a son of the Stockmann's great brindle Champion Rolf v. Vogelsberg. Rolf was recognized on a Munich street as a superlative specimen and was immediately purchased by a doctor who, in turn, sold him to the Stockmanns. Although Rolf left for war duty at the age of six and did not return until he was eleven, he left behind progeny that became the foundation of the von Dom strain.

WHERE DID DOGS COME FROM?

It can be argued that dogs were right there at man's side from the beginning of time. As soon as human beings began to document their existence, the dog was among their drawings and inscriptions. Dogs were not just friends, they served a purpose: There were dogs to hunt birds, pull sleds, herd sheep, burrow after rats—even sit in laps! What your dog was originally bred to do influences the way he behaves. The American Kennel Club recognizes over 140 breeds, and there are hundreds more distinct breeds around the world. To make sense of the breeds, they are grouped according to their size or function. The AKC has seven groups:

1. Sporting
2. Working
3. Herding
4. Hounds
5. Terriers
6. Toys
7. Non Sporting

Can you name a breed from each group? Here's some help: (1) Golden Retriever; (2) Doberman Pinscher; (3) Collie; (4) Beagle; (5) Scottish Terrier; (6) Maltese; and (7) Dalmatian. All modern domestic dogs *(Canis familiaris)* are related, however different they look, and are all descended from *Canis lupus,* the gray wolf.

Although the first Boxer to be registered in the U.S. was recorded by the AKC in 1904, Dampf became the first American Boxer champion in 1915.

PIONEERS IN THE BREED

There was a small but dedicated contingent of Boxer enthusiasts in America in the early years of this century. The American Boxer

It can be said that most modern Boxers probably trace back to one or more animals Mazelaine owned or bred.

Club itself, the breed's parent club in this country, was founded in 1935. These pioneering enthusiasts included G. J. Jeuther, who finished the championship of the second Boxer to attain a championship title in the U.S.: Ch. Bluecher v. Rosengarten. In 1931, Dr. Benjamin Birk imported German dogs as foundation stock for his Birkbaum kennels; in 1932, Marcia and Joseph Fennessey's Check v. Hennenstein finished as the third U.S. Boxer champion; and in 1933, Henry Stoecker of New Jersey finished Dodi v.d. Stoeckersburg, a brindle bitch who was the first female champion in the U.S. and the first to be whelped (born) in America, though she was German bred as her dam had come to this country in whelp.

In 1934, Mr. Stoecker finished Lord v.d. Stoeckersburg, who was the first American-bred champion and a half brother to Dodi out of the same dam. In 1936, the AKC moved Boxers from the Non Sporting to the Working Group. This occasioned considerable dismay among many fanciers who felt that the Boxer could not compete successfully against the popular Doberman or Collie. In time, however, their fears were to prove unfounded.

In 1938, Philip Stockman of Germany was invited to judge the American Boxer Club (ABC) Specialty. He awarded Best of Breed to the legendary Lustig. Herr Stockmann attended the ABC annual meeting that week, and his advice was sought in regard to the breed standard. One of his suggestions was that Boxers who were over one-third white be disqualified. Although at least one "Check" had by that time finished his U.S. championship, the ABC adopted the disqualification provision. It stands today.

The Mazelaine Kennels

From 1934 to 1964, John and Mazie Wagner of Wisconsin bred or owned 123 champions under the banner of their Mazelaine Kennels. They were responsible for the importation of two of the great foundation sires of the breed: Dorian (sire of forty champions) and Utz (sire of thirty-seven champions).

The Wagners were blessed with a rare combination of talents: a real appreciation of breed type and a scientific understanding of the best ways to produce it. The genetic prepotence their dogs left behind was of singular importance in the breed, and it can be said that most modern Boxers today probably trace back to one or more animals Mazelaine owned or bred.

FLASHY AND FANCY

On February 17, 1949, a flashy fawn puppy bred and owned by Mr. and Mrs. R. C. Harris was whelped at their Sirrah Crest Kennels in California. He grew up to be the incomparable Ch. Bang Away of Sirrah Crest, winner of 121 all-breed Best in Shows and sire of eighty-one U.S. champions.

ALL ABOUT BANG AWAY

No other Boxer whelped before or since has come close to approximating his stunning record as a show dog or a producer. Almost every living Boxer descends from Bang Away; his prepotence was ensured, as he left behind no fewer than seven ABC designated Sires and Dams of Merit. (In order to be a Sire or Dam of Merit, a Sire must produce at least seven champions and a Dam must produce at least four.)

Bang Away's showmanship was legendary, and it was evidenced very early—at only 10 weeks of age, he was chosen Best in Match out of ninety puppies judged by Frau Stockmann herself, visiting in California. Bang Away was Winners Dog and Best of Winners (meaning he was best of all the entrants except those who had already earned championship titles) from the 9–12 Puppy class at the 1950 ABC Specialty show.

FAMOUS OWNER'S OF THE BOXER

Elvis Presley

Shirley Temple

Humphrey Bogart

Lauren Bacall

Nat King Cole

Joan Crawford

Sylvester Stallone

Ice-T

In 1951, Bang Away achieved the great distinction of being Best in Show at the Westminster Kennel Club at Madison Square Garden. He was the third Boxer to go to the top at the Garden. The others were Ch. Warlord of Mazelaine (1947) and Ch. Mazelaine's Zazarac Brandy (1949). The next Boxer to win Westminster would have to wait almost twenty years: Ch. Arriba's Prima Donna (1970).

Bang Away was a flashy Boxer, meaning he had a striking amount of white on his face and feet. Until his day, Boxers in America tended to be "plainer," marked with less white. The love affair with "flash" continues into the 1990s.

BECOMING POPULAR

The popularity of the Boxer in America surged in the 1950s. It seemed like everywhere you looked someone was walking a Boxer down the street.

Press coverage of the three Madison Square Garden wins, plus the Boxer's natural virtues of medium size and a short and tidy haircoat, contributed to his popularity. In addition, it was becoming well-publicized that while he remained an excellent guard and watchdog, he was inordinately fond of children and a friend to almost all who approached him with good intentions. He was ranked number two in all breed registrations in 1955 and 1956.

Of course, all this attention rarely does a breed any lasting good, and the Boxer fell victim to "backyard" breeders out to make a fast dollar. Both health and temperament suffered as a result. However, those dedicated breeders who truly loved and admired the Boxer kept patiently breeding quality animals, and the public's mercurial tastes thankfully turned to other breeds.

THE 1960S TO THE PRESENT

The period of the 1960s and early '70s saw breeders developing and refining the Boxer. Their work has contributed to the taller, higher-stationed animal as we know him today. Not everyone agreed with the trends, but they are facts, nonetheless.

The Salgray Kennels

The Salgray Kennels of Daniel and Phyllis Hamilburg of Massachusetts

gave the Boxer new elegance and style, and they must be considered important architects in creating this "new" Boxer.

Salgray Boxers and their descendants changed the way many looked at the breed then and now. They were, in general, taller, more refined and more elegant than the breed had been in its infancy in America.

It is not surprising that the Boxer's guard- and watchdog abilities along with his love of people make him a popular breed.

Kennels all over the world have contributed to the development of the Boxer.

The Hamilburg's daughter, Jane Guy, continues to breed the Salgray line to this day.

TODAY'S DOG

In the 1980s and '90s the Boxer has settled into comfortable AKC registration figures. In 1998, he ranked twelfth out of approximately 137 breeds. He continues to enjoy a quiet but devoted following, and indeed he has been owned by many famous "fans" over the years, including Elvis Presley, Humphrey Bogart, Broderick Crawford, Lauren Bacall and Shirley Temple.

The modern Boxer is a well-mannered service dog and beloved friend to all.

Happily, peacetime has not required him to act as a war dog, either
as sentry or message-taker, as was
common in both World Wars. Instead,
he has become a successful guide dog
for the blind, a certified specialist
trained to help the physically handicapped and a well-mannered visitor
bringing cheer to nursing homes.

A TRUE HOMEBODY

While the Boxer is an exciting
show dog, he is always happiest at
home with those he loves. Indeed
it is his loyalty and sweet disposi-
tion that have endeared him to
his legions of admirers over the
years.

CHAPTER EIGHT

On Good Behavior

Dr. Ian Dunbar, Ph.D., MRCVS

well-behaved and good-natured puppydog is always a joy to live with, but an untrained and uncivilized dog can be a perpetual nightmare. Moreover, deny the dog an education and she will not have the opportunity to fulfill her own canine potential; neither will she have the ability to communicate effectively with her human companions.

Luckily, modern psychological training methods are easy, efficient, effective and, above all, considerably dog-friendly and user-friendly. Doggy education is as simple as it is enjoyable. But before you can have a good time play-training with your new dog, you have to learn what to do and how to do it. There is no

T raining is the jewel in the crown— the most important aspect of doggy husbandry. There is no more important variable influencing dog behavior and temperament than the dog's education: A well-trained, bigger variable influencing the success of dog training than the owner's experience and expertise. Before you embark on the dog's education, you must first educate yourself.

BASIC TRAINING FOR OWNERS

Ideally, basic owner training should begin well before you select your dog. Find out all you can about your chosen breed first, then master rudimentary training and handling skills. If you already have your puppydog, owner training is a dire emergency—the clock is ticking! Especially for puppies, the first few weeks at home are the most important and influential days in the dog's life. Indeed, the cause of most adolescent and adult problems may be traced back to the initial days the pup explores her new home. This is the time to establish the *status quo*— to teach the puppydog how you would like her to behave and so prevent otherwise quite predictable problems.

In addition to consulting breeders and breed books such as this one (which understandably have a positive breed bias), seek out as many pet owners with your breed as you can find. Good points are obvious. What you want to find out are the breed-specific problems, so you can nip them in the bud. In particular, you should talk to owners with adolescent dogs and make a list of all anticipated problems. Most important, test drive at least half a dozen adolescent and adult dogs of your breed yourself. An 8-week-old puppy is deceptively easy to handle, but she will acquire adult size, speed and strength in just four months, so you should learn now what to prepare for.

Puppy and pet dog training classes offer a convenient venue to locate pet owners and observe dogs in action. For a list of suitable trainers in your area, contact the Association of Pet Dog Trainers (see chapter 9). You may also begin your basic owner training by observing other owners in class. Watch as many classes and test drive as many dogs as possible. Select an upbeat, dog-friendly, people-friendly, fun-and-games, puppydog pet training class to learn the ropes. Also, watch training videos and read training books. You must find out what to do and how to do it *before* you have to do it.

65

Knowing what to expect of your puppy prior to her arrival in your home is a great way to stop behavior problems before they start.

PRINCIPLES OF TRAINING

Most people think training comprises teaching the dog to do things such as sit, speak and roll over, but even a 4-week-old pup knows how to do these things already. Instead, the first step in training involves teaching the dog human words for each dog behavior and activity and for each aspect of the dog's environment. That way you, the owner, can more easily participate in the dog's domestic education by directing her to perform specific actions appropriately, that is, at the right time, in the right place and so on. Training opens communication channels, enabling an educated dog to at least understand her owner's requests.

In addition to teaching a dog what we want her to do, it is also necessary to teach her why she should do what we ask. Indeed, 95 percent of training revolves around motivating the dog to want to do what we want. Dogs often understand what their owners want; they just don't see the point of doing it—especially when the owner's repetitively boring and seemingly senseless instructions are totally at odds with much more pressing and exciting doggy distractions. It is not so much the dog that is being stubborn or dominant; rather, it is the owner who has failed to acknowledge the dog's needs and feelings and to approach training from the dog's point of view.

The Meaning of Instructions

The secret to successful training is learning how to use training lures to predict or prompt specific behaviors— to coax the dog to do what you want when you want. Any highly valued object (such as a treat or toy) may be used as a lure, which the dog will follow with her eyes and nose. Moving the lure in specific ways entices the dog to move her nose, head and entire body in specific ways. In fact, by learning the art of manipulating various lures, it is possible to teach the dog to assume virtually any body position and perform any action. Once you have control over the expression of the dog's behaviors and can elicit any body position or behavior at will, you can easily teach the dog to perform on request.

Tell your dog what you want her to do, use a lure to entice her to respond correctly, then profusely praise and maybe reward her once she performs the desired action. For example, verbally request "Fido, sit!" while you move a squeaky toy upwards and backwards over the dog's muzzle (lure-movement and hand signal), smile knowingly as she looks up (to follow the lure) and sits down (as a result of canine anatomical engineering), then praise her to distraction ("Gooood Fido!"). Squeak the toy, offer a training treat and give your

dog and yourself a pat on the back.

Being able to elicit desired responses over and over enables the owner to reward the dog over and over. Consequently, the dog begins to think training is fun. For example, the more the dog is rewarded for sitting, the more she enjoys sitting. Eventually the dog comes to realize

You can quickly train your dog to do virtually anything when using the lure-reward method, and it is enjoyable for dogs, too!

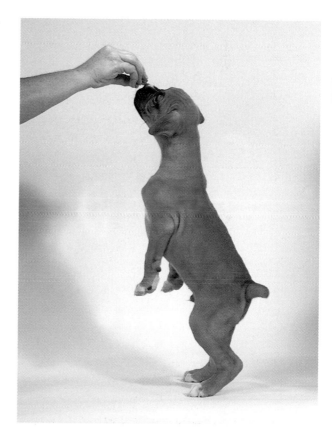

that, whereas most sitting is appreciated, sitting immediately upon request usually prompts especially enthusiastic praise and a slew of high-level rewards. The dog begins to sit on cue much of the time, showing that she is starting to grasp the meaning of the owner's verbal request and hand signal.

Why Comply?

Most dogs enjoy initial lure-reward training and are only too happy to comply with their owners' wishes. Unfortunately, repetitive drilling without appreciative feedback tends to diminish the dog's enthusiasm until she eventually fails to see the point of complying anymore. Moreover, as the dog approaches adolescence she becomes more easily distracted as she develops other interests. Lengthy sessions with repetitive exercises tend to bore and demotivate both parties. If it's not fun, the owner doesn't do it and neither does the dog.

Integrate training into your dog's life: The greater number of training sessions each day and the shorter they are, the more willingly compliant your dog will become. Make sure to

have a short (just a few seconds) training interlude before every enjoyable canine activity. For example, ask your dog to sit to greet people, to sit before you throw her Frisbee and to sit for her supper. Really, sitting is no different from a canine "Please." Also, include numerous short training interludes during every enjoyable canine pastime, for example, when playing with the dog or when she is running in the park. In this fashion, doggy distractions may be effectively converted into rewards for training. Just as all games have rules, fun becomes training . . . and training becomes fun.

Eventually, rewards actually become unnecessary to continue motivating your dog. If trained with consideration and kindness, performing the desired behaviors will become self-rewarding and, in a sense, your dog will motivate herself. Just as it is not necessary to reward a human companion during an enjoyable walk in the park, or following a game of tennis, it is hardly necessary to reward our best friend—the dog—for walking by our side or while playing fetch. Human company during enjoyable activities is reward enough for most dogs.

Even though your dog has become self-motivating, it's still good to praise and pet her a lot and offer rewards once in a while, especially for a job well done. And if for no other reason, praising and rewarding others is good for the human heart.

Punishment

Without a doubt, lure-reward training is by far the best way to teach: Entice your dog to do what you want and then reward her for doing so. Unfortunately, a human shortcoming is to take the good for granted and to moan and groan at the bad. Specifically, the dog's many good behaviors are ignored while the owner focuses on punishing the dog for making mistakes. In extreme cases, instruction is limited to punishing mistakes made by a trainee dog, child, employee or husband, even though it has been proven punishment training is notoriously inefficient and ineffective and is decidedly unfriendly and combative. It teaches the dog that training is a drag, almost as quickly as it teaches the dog to dislike her trainer. Why treat our best friends like our worst enemies?

Punishment training is also much more laborious and time-consuming. Whereas it takes only a finite amount of time to teach a dog what to chew, for example, it takes much, much longer to punish the dog for each and every mistake. Remember, there is only one right way! So why not teach that right way from the outset?!

To make matters worse, punishment training causes severe lapses in the dog's reliability. Since it is obviously impossible to punish the dog each and every time she misbehaves, the dog quickly learns to distinguish

When training your puppy, allow for frequent rests.

69

between those times when she must comply (so as to avoid impending punishment) and those times when she need not comply, because punishment is impossible. Such times include when the dog is off leash and 6 feet away, when the owner is otherwise engaged (talking to a friend, watching television, taking a shower, tending to the baby or chatting on the telephone) or when the dog is left at home alone.

Instances of misbehavior will be numerous when the owner is away, because even when the dog complied in the owner's looming presence, she did so unwillingly. The dog was forced to act against her will, rather than molding her will to want to please. Hence, when the owner is absent, not only does the dog know she need not comply, she simply does not want to. Again, the trainee is not a stubborn vindictive beast, but rather the trainer has failed to teach. Punishment training invariably creates unpredictable Jekyll and Hyde behavior.

TRAINER'S TOOLS

Many training books extol the virtues of a vast array of training paraphernalia and electronic and metallic gizmos, most of which are designed for canine restraint, correction and punishment, rather than for actual facilitation of doggy education. In reality, most effective training tools are not found in stores; they come from within ourselves. In addition to a willing dog, all you really need is a functional human brain, gentle hands, a loving heart and a good attitude.

In terms of equipment, all dogs do require a quality buckle collar to sport dog tags and to attach the leash (for safety and to comply with local leash laws). Hollow chew toys (like Kongs or sterilized longbones) and a dog bed or collapsible crate are musts for housetraining. Three additional tools are required:

1. specific lures (training treats and toys) to predict and prompt specific desired behaviors;

2. rewards (praise, affection, training treats and toys) to reinforce for the dog what a lot of fun it all is; and

3. knowledge—how to convert the dog's favorite activities and games (potential distractions to training) into "life-rewards," which may be employed to facilitate training.

The most powerful of these is knowledge. Education is the key! Watch training classes, participate in training classes, watch videos, read books, enjoy play-training with your dog and then your dog will say "Please," and your dog will say "Thank you!"

HOUSETRAINING

If dogs were left to their own devices, certainly they would chew, dig and bark for entertainment and then no doubt highlight a few areas of their living space with sprinkles of urine, in much the same way we decorate by hanging pictures. Consequently, when we ask a dog to live with us, we must teach her *where* she may dig, *where* she may perform her toilet duties, *what* she may chew and *when* she may bark. After all, when left at home alone for many hours, we cannot expect the dog to amuse herself by completing crosswords or watching TV!

Also, it would be decidedly unfair to keep the house rules a secret from the dog, and then get angry and punish the poor critter for inevitably transgressing rules she did not even know existed. Remember: Without adequate education and guidance, the dog will be forced to establish her own rules—doggy rules—and most probably will be at odds with the owner's view of domestic living.

Since most problems develop during the first few days the dog is at home, prospective dog owners must be certain they are quite clear about the principles of housetraining *before* they get a dog. Early misbehaviors quickly become established as the *status quo*—becoming firmly entrenched as hard-to-break bad habits, which set the precedent for years to come. Make sure to teach your dog good habits right from the start. Good habits are just as hard to break as bad ones!

HOUSETRAINING 1-2-3

1. Prevent mistakes. When you can't supervise your puppy, confine her in a single room or in her crate (but don't leave her for too long!). Puppy-proof the area by laying down newspapers so that if she does make a mistake, it won't matter.

2. Teach where. Take your puppy to the spot you want her to use every hour.

3. When she goes, praise her profusely and give her three favorite treats.

Ideally, when a new dog comes home, try to arrange for someone to be present as much as possible during the first few days (for adult dogs) or weeks for puppies. With only a little forethought, it is surprisingly easy to find a puppy sitter, such as a retired person, who would be willing to eat from your refrigerator and watch your television while keeping an eye on the newcomer to encourage the dog to play with chew toys and to ensure she goes outside on a regular basis.

Potty Training

Follow these steps to teach the dog where she should relieve herself:

1. never let her make a single mistake;

2. let her know where you want her to go; and

3. handsomely reward her for doing so: "GOOOOOOOD DOG!!!" liver treat, liver treat, liver treat!

Preventing Mistakes

A single mistake is a training disaster, since it heralds many more in future

weeks. And each time the dog soils the house, this further reinforces the dog's unfortunate preference for an indoor, carpeted toilet. Do not let an unhousetrained dog have full run of the house.

When you are away from home, or cannot pay full attention, confine the dog to an area where elimination is appropriate, such as an outdoor run or, better still, a small, comfortable indoor kennel with access to an outdoor run. When confined in this manner, most dogs will naturally housetrain themselves.

If that's not possible, confine the dog to an area, such as a utility room, kitchen, basement or garage, where elimination may not be desired in the long run but as an interim measure it is certainly preferable to doing it all around the house. Use newspaper to cover the floor of the dog's day room. The newspaper may be used to soak up the urine and to wrap up and dispose of the feces. Once your dog develops a preferred spot for eliminating, it is only necessary to cover that part of the floor with newspaper. The smaller papered area may then be moved (only a little each day) towards the door to the outside. Thus the dog will develop the tendency to go to the door when she needs to relieve herself.

Never confine an unhousetrained dog to a crate for long periods. Doing so would force the dog to soil the crate and ruin its usefulness as an aid for housetraining (see the following discussion).

Teaching Where

In order to teach your dog where you would like her to do her business, you have to be there to direct the proceedings—an obvious, yet often neglected, fact of life. In order to be there to teach the dog where to go, you need to know *when* she needs to go. Indeed, the success of housetraining depends on the owner's ability to predict these times. Certainly, a regular feeding schedule will facilitate prediction somewhat, but there is nothing like "loading the deck" and influencing the timing of the outcome yourself!

Whenever you are at home, make sure the dog is under constant supervision and/or confined to a small area. If already well trained, simply instruct the dog to lie down in her bed or basket. Alternatively, confine the dog to a crate (doggy den) or tie-down (a short, 18-inch lead that can be clipped to an eye hook in the baseboard near her bed). Short-term close confinement strongly inhibits urination and defecation, since the dog does not want to soil her sleeping area. Thus, when you release the puppydog each hour, she will definitely need to urinate immediately and defecate every third or fourth hour. Keep the dog confined to her doggy den and take her to her intended toilet area each hour, every hour and on the hour. When taking your dog outside, instruct her to sit quietly before opening the door— she will soon learn to sit by the door when she needs to go out!

Teaching Why

Being able to predict when the dog needs to go enables the owner to be on the spot to praise and reward the dog. Each hour, hurry the dog to the intended toilet area in the yard, issue the appropriate instruction ("Go pee!" or "Go poop!"), then give the dog three to four minutes to produce. Praise and offer a couple of training treats when successful. The treats are important because many people fail to praise their dogs with feeling . . .

and housetraining is hardly the time for understatement. So either loosen up and enthusiastically praise that dog: "Wuzzer-wuzzer-wuzzer, hoooser good wuffer den? Hoooo went pee for Daddy?" Or say "Good dog!" as best you can and offer the treats for effect.

Following elimination is an ideal time for a spot of play-training in the yard or house. Also, an empty dog may be allowed greater freedom around the house for the next half hour or so, just as long as you keep an eye out to make sure she does not get into other kinds of mischief. If you are preoccupied and cannot pay full attention, confine the dog to her doggy den once more to enjoy a peaceful snooze or to play with her many chew toys.

If your dog does not eliminate within the allotted time outside—no biggie! Back to her doggy den, and then try again after another hour.

As I own large dogs, I always feel more relaxed walking an empty dog, knowing that I will not need to finish our stroll weighted down with bags of feces!

Beware of falling into the trap of walking the dog to get her to eliminate. The good ol' dog walk is such an enormous highlight in the dog's life that it represents the single biggest potential reward in domestic dogdom. However, when in a hurry, or during inclement weather, many owners abruptly terminate the walk the moment the dog has done her business. This, in effect, severely punishes the dog for doing the right thing, in the right place at the right time. Consequently, many dogs become strongly inhibited from eliminating outdoors because they know it will signal an abrupt end to an otherwise thoroughly enjoyable walk.

Instead, instruct the dog to relieve herself in the yard prior to going for a walk. If you follow the above instructions, most dogs soon learn to eliminate on cue. As soon as the dog eliminates, praise (and offer a treat or two)—"Good dog! Let's go walkies!" Use the walk as a reward for eliminating in the yard. If the dog does not go, put her back in her doggy den and think about a walk later on. You will find with a "No feces—no walk" policy, your dog will become one of the fastest defecators in the business.

If you do not have a backyard, instruct the dog to eliminate right outside your front door prior to the walk.

Not only will this facilitate clean up and disposal of the feces in your own trash can but, also, the walk may again be used as a colossal reward.

CHEWING AND BARKING

Short-term close confinement also teaches the dog that occasional quiet moments are a reality of domestic living. Your puppydog is extremely impressionable during her first few weeks at home. Regular confinement at this time soon exerts a calming influence over the dog's personality. Remember, once the dog is housetrained and calmer, there will be a whole lifetime ahead for the dog to enjoy full run of the house and garden. On the other hand, by letting the newcomer have unrestricted access to the entire household and allowing her to run willy-nilly, she will most certainly develop a bunch of behavior problems in short order, no doubt necessitating confinement later in life. It would not be fair to remedially restrain and confine a dog you have trained, through neglect, to run free.

When confining the dog, make sure she always has an impressive array of suitable chew toys. Kongs and

Teaching your puppy to play with lots of fun toys will keep her from chewing up your shoes, and will certainly remain your pet's favorite hobby into her adult years.

TOYS THAT EARN THEIR KEEP

To entertain even the most distracted of dogs, while you're home or away, have a selection of the following toys on hand: hollow chew toys (like Kongs, sterilized hollow longbones and cubes or balls that can be stuffed with kibble). Smear peanut butter or honey on the inside of the hollow toy or bone and stuff the bone with kibble and your dog will think of nothing else but working the object to get at the food. Great to take your dog's mind off the fact that you've left the house.

sterilized longbones (both readily available from pet stores) make the best chew toys, since they are hollow and may be stuffed with treats to heighten the dog's interest. For example, by stuffing the little hole at the top of a Kong with a small piece of freeze-dried liver, the dog will not want to leave it alone.

Remember, treats do not have to be junk food and they certainly should not represent extra calories. Rather, treats should be part of each dog's regular daily diet: Some food may be served in the dog's bowl for breakfast and dinner, some food may be used as training treats, and some food may be used for stuffing chew toys. I regularly stuff my dogs' many Kongs with different shaped biscuits and kibble. The kibble seems to fall out fairly easily, as do the oval-shaped biscuits, thus rewarding the dog instantaneously for checking out the chew toys. The bone-shaped biscuits fall out after a while, rewarding the dog for worrying at the chew toy. But the triangular biscuits never come out. They remain inside the Kong as lures, maintaining the dog's fascination with her chew toy. To further focus the dog's interest, I always make sure to flavor the triangular biscuits by rubbing them with a little cheese or freeze-dried liver.

If stuffed chew toys are reserved especially for times the dog is confined, the puppydog will soon learn to enjoy quiet moments in her doggy den and she will quickly develop a chew-toy habit—a good habit! This is a simple autoshaping process; all the owner has to do is set up the situation and the dog all but trains herself—easy and effective. Even when the dog is given run of the house, her first inclination will be to indulge her rewarding chew-toy habit rather than destroy less-attractive household articles, such as curtains, carpets, chairs and compact disks. Similarly, a chew-toy chewer will be less inclined to scratch and chew herself excessively. Also, if the dog busies herself as a recreational chewer, she will be less inclined to develop into a recreational barker or digger when left at home alone.

Stuff a number of chew toys whenever the dog is left confined and remove the extra-special-tasting treats when you return. Your dog will now amuse herself with her chew toys before falling asleep and then resume playing with her chew toys when she expects you to return. Since most owner-absent misbehavior happens right after you leave and right before your expected return, your puppydog will now be conveniently preoccupied with her chew toys at these times.

COME AND SIT

Most puppies will happily approach virtually anyone, whether called or not; that is, until they collide with adolescence and develop other more important doggy interests, such as sniffing a multiplicity of exquisite odors on the grass. Your mission,

Mr./Ms. Owner, is to teach and reward the pup for coming reliably, willingly and happily when called— and you have just three months to get it done. Unless adequately reinforced, your puppy's tendency to approach people will self-destruct by adolescence.

Call your dog ("Fido, come!"), open your arms (and maybe squat down) as a welcoming signal, waggle a treat or toy as a lure and reward the puppydog when she comes running. Do not wait to praise the dog until she reaches you—she may come 95 percent of the way and then run off after some distraction. Instead, praise the dog's first step towards you and continue praising enthusiastically for every step she takes in your direction.

When the rapidly approaching puppy dog is three lengths away from impact, instruct her to sit ("Fido, sit!") and hold the lure in front of you in an outstretched hand to prevent her from hitting you mid-chest and knocking you flat on your back! As Fido decelerates to nose the lure, move the treat upwards and backwards just over her muzzle with an upwards motion of your extended arm (palm-upwards). As the dog looks up to follow the lure, she will sit down (if she jumps up, you are holding the lure too high). Praise the dog for sitting. Move backwards and call her again. Repeat this many times over, always praising when Fido comes and sits; on occasion, reward her.

For the first couple of trials, use a training treat both as a lure to entice the dog to come and sit and as a reward for doing so. Thereafter, try to use different items as lures and rewards. For example, lure the dog with a Kong or Frisbee but reward her with a food treat. Or lure the dog with a food treat but pat her and throw a tennis ball as a reward. After just a few repetitions, dispense with the lures and rewards; the dog will begin to respond willingly to your verbal requests and hand signals just for the prospect of praise from your heart and affection from your hands.

Instruct every family member, friend and visitor how to get the dog to come and sit. Invite people over for a series of pooch parties; do not keep the pup a secret—let other people enjoy this puppy, and let the pup enjoy other people. Puppydog parties are not only fun, they easily attract a lot of people to help you train your dog. Unless you teach your dog how to meet people, that is, to sit for greetings, no doubt the dog will resort to jumping up. Then you and the visitors will get annoyed, and the dog will be punished. This is not fair. Send out those invitations for puppy parties and teach your dog to be mannerly and socially acceptable.

Even though your dog quickly masters obedient recalls in the house, her reliability may falter when playing in the backyard or local park. Ironically, it is the owner who has unintentionally trained the dog not to respond in these instances. By allowing the dog to play and run around and otherwise have a good time, but then to call the dog to put her on leash to take her home, the dog quickly learns playing is fun but training is a drag. Thus, playing in the park becomes a severe distraction, which works against training. Bad news!

Instead, whether playing with the dog off leash or on leash, request her to come at frequent intervals— say, every minute or so. On most occasions, praise and pet the dog for a few seconds while she is sitting, then tell her to go play again. For especially fast recalls, offer a couple of training treats and take the time to praise and pet the dog enthusiastically before releasing her. The dog will learn that coming when called is not necessarily the end of the play session, and neither is it the end of the world; rather, it signals an enjoyable, quality time-out with the owner before resuming play once more. In fact, playing in the park now becomes a very effective life-reward, which works to facilitate training by reinforcing each obedient and timely recall. Good news!

SIT, DOWN, STAND AND ROLLOVER

Teaching the dog a variety of body positions is easy for owner and dog, impressive for spectators and extremely useful for all. Using lure-reward techniques, it is possible to train several positions at once to verbal commands or hand signals (which impress the socks off onlookers).

Sit and down—the two control commands—prevent or resolve nearly a hundred behavior problems. For example, if the dog happily and obediently sits or lies down when requested,

79

This Boxer has learned the sit and stay commands.

she cannot jump on visitors, dash out the front door, run around and chase her tail, pester other dogs, harass cats or annoy family, friends or strangers. Additionally, "Sit" or "Down" are the best emergency commands for off-leash control.

It is easier to teach and maintain a reliable sit than maintain a reliable recall. Sit is the purest and simplest of commands—either the dog is sitting or she is not. If there is any change of circumstances or potential danger in the park, for example, simply instruct the dog to sit. If she sits, you have a number of options: Allow the dog to resume playing when she is safe, walk up and put the dog on leash or call the dog. The dog will be much more likely to come when called if she has already acknowledged her compliance by sitting. If the dog does not sit in the park—train her to!

Stand and rollover-stay are the two positions for examining the dog. Your veterinarian will love you to distraction if you take a little time to teach the dog to stand still and roll over and play possum. Also, your vet bills will be smaller because it will take the veterinarian less time to examine your dog. The rollover-stay

is an especially useful command and is really just a variation of the down-stay: Whereas the dog lies prone in the traditional down, she lies supine in the rollover-stay.

As with teaching come and sit, the training techniques to teach the dog to assume all other body positions on cue are user-friendly and dog-friendly. Simply give the appropriate request, lure the dog into the desired body position using a training treat or toy and then praise (and maybe reward) the dog as soon as she complies. Try not to touch the dog to get her to respond. If you teach the dog by guiding her into position, the dog will quickly learn that rump-pressure means sit, for example, but as yet you still have no control over your dog if she is just 6 feet away. It will still be necessary to teach the dog to sit on request. So do not make training a time-consuming two-step process; instead, teach the dog to sit to a verbal request or hand signal from the outset. Once the dog sits willingly when requested, by all means use your hands to pet the dog when she does so.

To teach down when the dog is already sitting, say "Fido, down!", hold the lure in one hand (palm down) and lower that hand to the floor between the dog's forepaws. As the dog lowers her head to follow the lure, slowly move the lure away from the dog just a fraction (in front of her paws). The dog will lie down as she stretches her nose forward to follow the lure. Praise the dog when she does so. If the dog stands up, you pulled the lure away too far and too quickly.

When teaching the dog to lie down from the standing position, say "Down" and lower the lure to the floor as before. Once the dog has lowered her forequarters and assumed a play bow, gently and slowly move the lure towards the dog between her forelegs. Praise the dog as soon as her rear end plops down.

After just a couple of trials it will be possible to alternate sits and downs and have the dog energetically perform doggy push-ups. Praise the dog a lot, and after half a dozen or so push-ups reward the dog with a training treat or toy. You will notice the more energetically you move your arm—upwards (palm up) to get the dog to sit, and downwards (palm down) to get the dog to lie down— the more energetically the dog responds to your requests. Now try

OWNING A PARTY ANIMAL

It's a fact: The more of the world your puppy is exposed to, the more comfortable she'll be in it. Once your puppy's had her shots, start taking her everywhere with you. Encourage friendly interaction with strangers, expose her to different environments (towns, fields, beaches) and most important, enroll her in a puppy class where she'll get to play with other puppies. These simple, fun, shared activities will develop your pup into a confident socialite; reliable around other people and dogs.

training the dog in silence and you will notice she has also learned to respond to hand signals. Yeah! Not too shabby for the first session.

To teach stand from the sitting position, say "Fido, stand," slowly move the lure half a dog-length away from the dog's nose, keeping it at nose level, and praise the dog as she stands to follow the lure. As soon as the dog stands, lower the lure to just beneath the dog's chin to entice her to look down; otherwise she will stand and then sit immediately. To prompt the dog to stand from the down position, move the lure half a dog-length upwards and away from the dog, holding the lure at standing nose height from the floor.

Teaching rollover is best started from the down position, with the dog lying on one side, or at least with both hind legs stretched out on the same side. Say "Fido, bang!" and move the lure backwards and alongside the dog's muzzle to her elbow (on the side of her outstretched hind legs). Once the dog looks to the side and backwards, very slowly move the lure upwards to the dog's shoulder and backbone. Tickling the dog in the goolies (groin area) often invokes a reflex-raising of the hind leg as an appeasement gesture, which facilitates the tendency to roll over. If you move the lure too quickly and the dog jumps into the standing position, have patience and start again. As soon as the dog rolls onto her back, keep the lure stationary and mesmerize the dog with a relaxing tummy rub.

To teach rollover-stay when the dog is standing or moving, say "Fido, bang!" and give the appropriate hand signal (with index finger pointed and thumb cocked in true Sam Spade fashion), then in one fluid movement lure her to first lie down and then rollover-stay as above.

Teaching the dog to stay in each of the above four positions becomes a piece of cake after first teaching the dog not to worry at the toy or treat training lure. This is best accomplished by hand feeding dinner kibble. Hold a piece of kibble firmly in your hand and softly instruct "Off!" Ignore any licking and slobbering for however long the dog worries at the treat, but say "Take it!" and offer the kibble the instant the dog breaks contact with her muzzle. Repeat this a few times, and then up the ante and insist the dog remove her muzzle for one whole second before offering the kibble. Then progressively refine your criteria and have the dog not touch your hand (or treat) for longer and longer periods on each trial, such as for two seconds, four seconds, then six, ten, fifteen, twenty, thirty seconds and so on.

The dog soon learns: (1) worrying at the treat never gets results, whereas (2) noncontact is often rewarded after a variable time lapse.

Teaching "Off!" has many useful applications in its own right. Additionally, instructing the dog not to touch a training lure often produces spontaneous and magical stays. Request the dog to stand-stay, for example, and not to touch the lure. At first set your sights on a short two-second stay before rewarding the dog. (Remember, every long journey begins with a single step.) However, on subsequent trials, gradually and progressively increase the length of stay required to receive a reward. In no time at all your dog will stand calmly for a minute or so.

RELEVANCY TRAINING

Once you have taught the dog what you expect her to do when requested to come, sit, lie down, stand, rollover and stay, the time is right to teach the dog why she should comply with your wishes. The secret is to have many (many) extremely short training interludes (two to five seconds each) at numerous (numerous) times during the course of the dog's day. Especially work with the dog immediately before the dog's good times and during the dog's good times. For example, ask your dog to sit and/or lie down each time before opening doors, serving meals, offering treats and tummy rubs; ask the dog to perform a few controlled doggy

Going for a walk is a great way to exercise and bond with your dog— and to train!

push-ups before letting her off leash or throwing a tennis ball; and perhaps request the dog to sit-down-sit-stand-down-stand-rollover before inviting her to cuddle on the couch.

Similarly, request the dog to sit many times during play or on walks, and in no time at all the dog will be only too pleased to follow your instructions because she has learned that a compliant response heralds all sorts of goodies. Basically all you are trying to teach the dog is how to say please: "Please throw the tennis ball. Please may I snuggle on the couch."

It is important to keep training interludes short and to have many short sessions each and every day. The shortest (and most useful) session comprises asking the dog to sit and then go play during a play session. When trained this way, your dog will soon associate training with good times. In fact, the dog may be unable to distinguish between training and good times and, indeed, there should be no distinction. The warped concept that training involves forcing the dog to comply and/or dominating her will is totally at odds with the picture of a truly well-trained dog. In reality, enjoying a game of training with a

dog is no different from enjoying a game of backgammon or tennis with a friend; and walking with a dog should be no different from strolling with a spouse, or with buddies on the golf course.

WALK BY YOUR SIDE

Many people attempt to teach a dog to heel by putting her on a leash and physically correcting the dog when she makes mistakes. There are a number of things seriously wrong with this approach, the first being that most people do not want precision heeling; rather, they simply want the dog to follow or walk by their side. Second, when physically restrained during "training," even though the dog may grudgingly mope by your side when "handcuffed" on leash, let's see what happens when she is off leash. History! The dog is in the next county because she never enjoyed walking with you on leash and you have no control over her off leash. So let's just teach the dog off leash from the outset to want to walk with us. Third, if the dog has not been trained to heel, it is a trifle hasty to think about punishing the poor dog for making mistakes and breaking heeling rules she didn't even know existed. This is simply not fair! Surely, if the dog had been adequately taught how to heel, she would seldom make mistakes and hence there would be no need to correct the dog. Remember, each mistake and each correction (punishment) advertise the trainer's inadequacy, not the dog's. The dog is not stubborn, she is not stupid and she is not bad. Even if she were, she would still require training, so let's train her properly.

Let's teach the dog to enjoy following us so she will want to walk by our side off leash. Then it will be easier to teach high-precision off-leash heeling patterns if desired. Before going on outdoor walks, it is necessary to teach the dog not to pull. Then it becomes easy to teach on-leash walking and heeling because the dog already wants to walk with you, she is familiar with the desired walking and heeling positions and she knows not to pull.

FOLLOWING

Start by training your dog to follow you. Many puppies will follow if you simply walk away from them and maybe click your fingers or chuckle. Adult dogs may require additional enticement to stimulate them to follow, such as a training lure or, at the very least, a lively trainer. To teach the dog to follow: (1) keep walking and (2) walk away from the dog. If the dog attempts to lead or lag, change pace; slow down if the dog forges too far ahead, but speed up if she lags too far behind. Say "Steady!" or "Easy!" each time before you slow down and

A well-trained Boxer will walk easily and calmly by your side.

85

FINDING A TRAINER

Have fun with your dog, take a training class! But don't just sign on any dotted line, find a trainer whose approach and style you like and whose students (and their dogs) are really learning. Ask to visit a class to observe a trainer in action. For the names of trainers near you, ask your veterinarian, your pet supply store, your dog-owning neighbors or call (800) PET-DOGS (the Association of Pet Dog Trainers).

If your Boxer pulls on leash, be sure to not pull back and to praise her when she finally sits still.

"Quickly!" or "Hustle!" each time before you speed up, and the dog will learn to change pace on cue. If the dog lags or leads too far, or if she wanders right or left, simply walk quickly in the opposite direction and maybe even run away from the dog and hide.

Practicing is a lot of fun; you can set up a course in your home, yard or park to do this. Indoors, entice the dog to follow upstairs, into a bedroom, into the bathroom, downstairs, around the living room couch, zigzagging between dining room chairs and into the kitchen for dinner. Outdoors, get the dog to follow around park benches, trees, shrubs and along walkways and lines in the grass. (For safety outdoors, it is advisable to attach a long line on the dog, but never exert corrective tension on the line.)

Remember, following has a lot to do with attitude—your attitude! Most probably your dog will not want to follow Mr. Grumpy Troll with the personality of wilted lettuce. Lighten up—walk with a jaunty step, whistle a happy tune, sing, skip and tell jokes to your dog and she will be right there by your side.

CHAPTER NINE

Resources

BOOKS

About Boxers

Hutchings, Tim. *The Complete Boxer.* New York: Howell Book House, 1998.

McFadden, Billie. *The New Boxer.* New York: Howell Book House, 1989.

Nicholas, Anna Katherine. *The Boxer.* Neptune, N.J.: TFH Publications, 1985.

Tomita, Richard. *The World of the Boxer.* Neptune, N.J.: TFH Publications, 1998.

About Health Care

American Kennel Club. *American Kennel Club Dog Care and Training.* New York: Howell Book House, 1991.

Carlson, Delbert, DVM, and James Giffen, MD. *Dog Owner's Home Veterinary Handbook.* New York: Howell Book House, 1992.

DeBitetto, James, DVM, and Sarah Hodgson. *You & Your Puppy.* New York: Howell Book House, 1995.

Lane, Marion. *The Humane Society of the United States Complete Guide to Dog Care.* New York: Little, Brown & Co., 1998.

McGinnis, Terri. *The Well Dog Book.* New York: Random House, 1991.

Schwartz, Stephanie, DVM. *First Aid for Dogs: An Owner's Guide to a Happy Healthy Pet.* New York: Howell Book House, 1998.

Volhard, Wendy and Kerry L. Brown. *The Holistic Guide for a Healthy Dog.* New York: Howell Book House, 1995.

About Training

Ammen, Amy. *Training in No Time.* New York: Howell Book House, 1995.

Benjamin, Carol Lea. *Mother Knows Best.* New York: Howell Book House, 1985.

Bohnenkamp, Gwen. *Manners for the Modern Dog.* San Francisco: Perfect Paws, 1990.

Dunbar, Ian, Ph.D., MRCVS. *Dr. Dunbar's Good Little Book.* James & Kenneth Publishers, 2140 Shattuck Ave. #2406, Berkeley, CA 94704. (510) 658-8588. Order from Publisher.

Evans, Job Michael. *People, Pooches and Problems.* New York: Howell Book House, 1991.

Palika, Liz. *All Dogs Need Some Training.* New York: Howell Book House, 1997.

Volhard, Jack and Melissa Bartlett. *What All Good Dogs Should Know: The Sensible Way to Train.* New York: Howell Book House, 1991.

About Activities

Hall, Lynn. *Dog Showing for Beginners.* New York: Howell Book House, 1994.

O'Neil, Jackie. *All About Agility.* New York: Howell Book House, 1998.

Simmons-Moake, Jane. *Agility Training, The Fun Sport for All Dogs.* New York: Howell Book House, 1991.

Vanacore, Connie. *Dog Showing: An Owner's Guide.* New York: Howell Book House, 1990.

Volhard, Jack and Wendy. *The Canine Good Citizen.* New York: Howell Book House, 1994.

MAGAZINES

THE AKC GAZETTE, The Official Journal for the Sport of Purebred Dogs
American Kennel Club
260 Madison Ave.
New York, NY 10016
www.akc.org

DOG FANCY
Fancy Publications
3 Burroughs
Irvine, CA 92618
(714) 855-8822
http://dogfancy.com

DOG & KENNEL
7-L Dundas Circle
Greensboro, NC 27407
(336) 292-4047
www.dogandkennel.com

DOG WORLD
Maclean Hunter Publishing Corp.
500 N. Dearborn, Ste. 1100
Chicago, IL 60610
(312) 396-0600
www.dogworldmag.com

PETLIFE: Your Companion Animal Magazine
Magnolia Media Group
1400 Two Tandy Center
Fort Worth, TX 76102
(800) 767-9377
www.petlifeweb.com

MORE INFORMATION ABOUT BOXERS

National Breed Club

AMERICAN BOXER CLUB, INC.
Corresponding Secretary:
    Barbara E. Wagner
    6310 Edward Dr.
    Clinton, MD 20735-4135

Breeder Contact:
    Lucille Jackson
    11300 Oakton Rd.
    Oakton, VA 22124
    (703) 385-9385
Breed Rescue:
    Connie Back
    (504) 738-5820

The Club can send you information on all aspects of the breed including the names and addresses of breed clubs in your area, as well as obedience clubs. Inquire about membership.

The American Kennel Club

The American Kennel Club (AKC), devoted to the advancement of purebred dogs, is the oldest and largest registry organization in this country. Every breed recognized by the AKC has a national (parent) club. National clubs are a great source of information on your breed. The affiliated clubs hold AKC events and use AKC rules to hold performance events, dog shows, educational programs, health clinics and training classes. The AKC staff is divided between offices in New York City and Raleigh, North Carolina. The AKC has an excellent Web site that provides information on the organization and all AKC-recognized breeds. The address is **www.akc.org**.

For registration and performance events information, or for customer service, contact:

THE AMERICAN KENNEL CLUB
5580 Centerview Dr., Suite 200
Raleigh, NC 27606
(919) 233-9767

The AKC's executive offices and the AKC Library (open to the public) are at this address:

THE AMERICAN KENNEL CLUB
260 Madison Ave.
New York, NY 10016
(212) 696-8200 (general information)
(212) 696-8246 (AKC Library)
www.akc.org

UNITED KENNEL CLUB
100 E. Kilgore Rd.
Kalamazoo, MI 49001-5598
(616) 343-9020
www.ukcdogs.com

AMERICAN RARE BREED ASSOCIATION
9921 Frank Tippett Rd.
Cheltenham, MD 20623
(301) 868-5718 (voice or fax)
www.arba.org

CANADIAN KENNEL CLUB
89 Skyway Ave., Ste. 100
Etobicoke, Ontario
Canada M9W 6R4
(416) 675-5511
www.ckc.ca

ORTHOPEDIC FOUNDATION FOR ANIMALS (OFA)
2300 E. Nifong Blvd.
Columbia, MO 65201-3856
(314) 442-0418
www.offa.org/

Trainers

Animal Behavior & Training Associates (ABTA)
9018 Balboa Blvd., Ste. 591
Northridge, CA 91325
(800) 795-3294
www.Good-dawg.com

Association of Pet Dog Trainers (APDT)
(800) PET-DOGS
www.apdt.com

National Association of Dog Obedience Instructors (NADOI)
729 Grapevine Highway, Ste. 369
Hurst, TX 76054-2085
www.kimberly.uidaho.edu/nadoi

Associations

Delta Society
P.O. Box 1080
Renton, WA 98507-1080
(Promotes the human/animal bond
through pet-assisted therapy and other
programs)
**www.petsforum.com/DELTASOCIETY/
dsi400.htm**

Dog Writers Association of America
(DWAA)
Sally Cooper, Secretary
222 Woodchuck Lane
Harwinton, CT 06791
www.dwaa.org

National Association for Search and
Rescue (NASAR)
4500 Southgate Place, Ste. 100
Chantilly, VA 20157
(703) 222-6277
www.nasar.org

Therapy Dogs International
6 Hilltop Rd.
Mendham, NJ 07945

OTHER USEFUL RESOURCES— WEB SITES

General Information— Links to Additional Sites, On-Line Shopping

www.k9web.com – resources for the dog
world
www.netpet.com – pet related products,
software and services
www.apapets.com – The American Pet
Association

www.dogandcatbooks.com – book
catalogue
www.dogbooks.com – on-line bookshop
www.animal.discovery.com/ – cable
television channel on-line

Health

www.avma.org – American Veterinary
Medical Association (AVMA)
www.aplb.org – Association for Pet Loss
Bereavement (APLB)—contains an
index of national hot lines for on-line
and office counseling
**www.netfopets.com/AskTheExperts.
html** – veterinary questions answered
on-line

Breed Information

www.bestdogs.com/news/ – newsgroup
www/cheta.net/connect/canine/breeds/
– Canine Connections Breed Information Index